The Love Triangle

Affirmation, Advocacy and Acceptance in Philemon

The Love Triangle

Affirmation, Advocacy and Acceptance in Philemon

Lance Moncrieffe

Copyright © 2025 Orlando Moncrieffe

All rights reserved.

No part of this book may be reproduced or transmitted in any form or by any means, electronic or mechanical, including photocopying, recording, or by any information storage or retrieval system, without permission in writing from the publisher.

ISBN: 979-8-9939000-1-8

Dedicated to my wife Abigail
(my prayer rock and best friend),
and to my father,
Dr. Orlando Moncrieffe, who
has unswervingly demonstrated
how to love the lost son and
return him to God.

Edited by Davya DiLauro

Table of Contents

PART ONE: RECOVERY

Chapter One — Set Free   3
Slavery   4
Denouncing Slavery   4
Encouraging The Discouraged   7
Slavery To Sin   10
The Son's Freedom   11

Chapter Two — The Emotional Triangle   15
The Runaway   15
The Safe Preacher   16
The Language Of Love   18
The Christian Servant   21
Restoration   22
The Christian Dilemma   27
Rollercoaster   28

PART TWO: LOVED

Chapter Three — My Son Whom I Love   37
Unimagined Love   37
Adoption   41
The Joy Of Belonging   48
Loving Advocacy   51

Chapter Four — Valuable Now   59
Profit And Loss   59
Rewired   61
Choreographed   67
Divine Confidence   69
Reappraisal   71

Chapter Five — My Heart   75
Poured Out   75
Entwined   78
Special To Me   81
The Missing Part   84
A Softened Heart   87

PART THREE: HOME

Chapter Six — Home Forever   95
Departure   96
The Silent Exodus   97
Divine Choice   99
Seasons   106
Fixed   108
Eternity   109
Forever Love   112

Chapter Seven — In The Family Now   117
Family Circle   117
From Stranger To Son   120
Above A Servant   124
Brother Beloved   128
Partner   130

PART FOUR: RELEASE

Chapter Eight — Charge That To My Account 139
The Transfer   139
The Acquittal   144
Hand-Written   146
My Blood   150
Living Peace   155

Chapter Nine — My own Letter Of Love   161

BIBLE TRANSLATION ABBREVIATIONS

Amplified Bible (AMP)

Berean Study Bible (BSB)

Christian English Version (CEV)

Christian Standard Bible (CSB)

English Standard Version (ESV)

King James Version (KJV)

Lamsa Bible (La)

Legacy Standard Bible (LSB)

New International Version (NIV)

New King James Version (NKJV)

New Living Translation (NLT)

Message Bible (MSG)

Smith's Literal Translation (SLT)

Webster's Bible Translation (WBT)

Word English Bible (WEB)

ACKNOWLEDGMENTS

Dr. Gary Banks, my 'iron sharpeneth iron' brother who among so many other things, taught me the powerful ministry of presence. Special gratitude for his thoughtful review of the 'Set Free' chapter of this writing.

Dr. Pete Palmer, (past President of the Allegheny East Conference of Seventh-day Adventists). My decades long friend and mentor who has carved my ministry in thought more than any other. Extremely thankful for his 'Neural Pathways' contribution to this writing.

W. Nick Taliaferro, (retired Pastor and radio personality). My mentor and friend who has taught me the real essence of pastoral life — love. I am indebted to his unknowing lessons of serving God's people without performance. My deep appreciation of his thoughtful review, guidance and foreword of this book cannot be suitably articulated.

FOREWORD
by W. Nick Taliaferro

Many readers of Scripture tend to treat the 25 verses of Paul's slender letter to Philemon as a textual whistle-stop. But in his new book, The Love Triangle, Pastor Lance Moncrieffe has turned this one-chapter treatise into a theological Grand Concourse on divine Love and Redemption.

Moncrieffe painstakingly unravels the nuanced layers of sociology, politics and theology woven throughout this brief letter between two friends (Paul and Philemon). Drawing out significant elements about how Divine Redemption works, he unpacks this story about a runaway, thieving slave, and reveals that it is a trenchant object lesson about restoration. In so doing, he includes all of us; revealing that we may all be, at one time or another, fugitives, or offended victims, or merchants of mercy.

The first chapter alone (Set Free) is worth the price of admission, as it examines the biblical/historical perspective on slavery. Moncrieffe deftly illuminates how the reality of enslavement in antiquity speaks to relevant social issues in our current world. While acknowledging "it is often easy to suggest (from our contextual social lens) that Paul doesn't go far enough on the issue of slavery…" we are taken deeper into the broader biblical perspective on how God values human beings, and how that might be more properly demonstrated in today's world.

But the book's deeper focus is found in its study on the relational aspect of redemption and salvation. In Philemon the Gospel is set forth as Love restoring broken relationships through forgiveness and the extending of uncommon mercy. Moncrieffe examines the pain and discomfort involved in dealing with the complex web of offenses and injustices that interrupt healthy relationships; then challenges us to endure them! The Love Triangle, almost therapeutically invites us all to investigate our own brokenness, and the breaches within relationships that we share, while also urging us to greater grace for the purpose of healing.

Paul's letter to Philemon offers a hopeful view for anyone who has endured the pain of broken relationships, or who may feel hopelessly beyond the reach of restoration. Better still, for those who may feel the outrage of having endured offense as innocent victims, Moncrieffe's work provides a call to transcend simply being right, and going on to become redemptively merciful.

PREFACE

There are thirteen epistles written by Paul the Apostle in the New Testament. These letters to churches and individuals are as varied in their content, purpose, and gravity as the needs of the recipients and their regions were. Amongst these epistles is a gorgeous little letter — with a tremendous message. It is a personal letter from Paul to his close friend Philemon — gracefully providing him affirmation of his spiritual walk, a fresh perspective on an old problem, and an opportunity for further spiritual growth.

And of course, the letter we're reflecting on is the book of Philemon. It is the shortest of all Paul's epistles, but it is among his most powerful and profound writings. Nestled within its ephemeral twenty-five verses, we find an emotionally rich relational triangle of love, trust, expectance, frustration, provision, deceit, theft, loss, anger, estrangement, loneliness, fear, guilt, compassion, acceptance, grace, conversion, adoption, hope, faith, transformation, optimism, advocacy, and salvation.

It is the full gospel in the most petite and poetically elegant form in the Bible. In it is summarized the love of God, the waywardness of the sinner, and the salvation of Christ. The relational dynamic between God, sinners, and Christ is projected onto the three main characters portrayed in the letter — Philemon the Master, Onesimus the runaway slave, and Paul the gospel preacher — who are all connected in a three-point relationship — a love triangle.

For us, the spiritual lessons become clear when we recognize these characters as the Biblical types they are. Philemon the master is a type of God: who had a servant rob Him and run away from His household and into the world. Onesimus the slave is a type of the sinner (like us): who runs away from our God, robs Him of our time, energies, effort, resources and talents; and quickly wastes it in the world. Paul is a type of Jesus Christ: who despite what city the sinner is lost or hiding in, He finds them where they are, comforts them, consoles them, feeds them, teaches them and converts them. And when they have become spiritually ready, He turns them around, points the way and sends them back, reuniting them with their master — God the Father.

The inclusion of this elegant letter in the sixty-six books of the Bible, extends its personal message of acceptance, transformation, and salvation beyond Paul's intended reader (Philemon), and onto each of us who read and absorb it today. From this letter we too can see how the love triangle is projected into our own lives. It provides us assurance that even today, our connection and relationship with Jesus Christ can reunite us back to God our Father.

PART ONE
RECOVERY

Chapter 1
SET FREE

Some have used the book of Philemon as Biblical support for slavery. The opposite is true. The Bible is unequivocal — slavery and slave trading in any form is sinful. The Bible is the Word of God, addressing the human need of salvation from sin. Slavery as a sin problem is captured within the scenes of the Biblical human story. As all sin in the Bible, it is identified, demonstrated, and finally overcome. There is no support for sin in God's Word.

In his letters to the churches in Galatia, Ephesus and Rome, along with his personal letter to Titus; we find Paul using familiar social concepts such as 'slavery' and 'adoption' as spiritual metaphors. These became powerful core pillars for Paul's gospel of 'salvation by faith', the 'grace of God', and 'transformation by the Holy Spirit'. While Paul doesn't intentionally feature 'slavery' and 'adoption' metaphorically in his letter to Philemon, it seems clear that it was written to a fellow Christian believer who was already conscious of these spiritual principles. A closer look at these social realities in Paul's time (especially slavery) will help us understand more of Paul's intended message, how it was received by Philemon and others, and what applications are relevant for our spiritual journey today.

Slavery

While addressing slavery itself wasn't the point, Paul used its existence as a platform for his message of love. True, the object of the letter was someone who was a slave. Equally true, the intended recipient of the letter was someone who owned slaves. Yet, this letter was not written to confront slavery itself. Paul does not use these few brief lines to tackle the large systemic and socially normalized evils of servitude in his day. But one should not take the absence of an open fight against slavery—in this letter—as an indication of Paul supporting slavery at all. We should take note that, if Paul's Christian request—of kindness, love, partnership, and freedom for Onesimus the slave—was accepted by Philemon his owner (and other Christian slave owners), it would naturally transform the owner/slave relationship and silently destabilize Greco-Roman slavery within Christian circles.

Denouncing Slavery

Paul's care for the enslaved persons of his day is seen in his writings. He addresses two forms of human slavery in his epistles: first, the kidnapping and sale of persons into forced servitude — which he denounces in the strongest of terms (1 Timothy 1:10); second, indentured (Leviticus 25:35-43) and chattel (Leviticus 25:44-46) slavery, where he encourages the enslaved to honor God through their Christian behavior while in bondage, yet urges them to seek freedom when an opportunity arises (1 Corinthians 7:21).

Paul addresses the evil of slavery head on in his first letter to his young pastor Timothy. As he advised Timothy on the type of challenges he would face in the church, Paul described people who buy and sell slaves (slave traders) as ungodly, sinful, unholy and irreligious (1 Timothy 1:10). The NIV translation renders the term 'slave traders'. The ESV uses the term 'enslavers'. The KJV translates the term as 'men-stealers'. The CEV expresses the term as 'kidnappers'. Neither translation misses Paul's personal and spiritual point — human theft, trafficking, forceful ownership, and involuntary servitude in any form is out of line with God's will.

The Greco-Roman world in Paul's day had a socially understood practice called man-stealing. An organized criminal system of kidnapping people for sale. Neither race, ethnicity, culture, age nor gender mattered to these men-stealers. Both the rich and the poor, the educated and the simple were potential victims in that barbaric system of enslavement. It is in this social context that Paul advises Timothy that those who engage in or benefit from slave trading are in direct opposition to God's will and the aspirational virtues of Christianity.

HUMAN THEFT, TRAFFICKING, FORCEFUL OWNERSHIP, AND INVOLUNTARY SERVITUDE IN ANY FORM IS OUT OF LINE WITH GOD'S WILL.

This wasn't simply Paul's New Testament era opinion. Paul was well versed in Old Testament (OT) laws, and understood that the kidnapping, sale, enslavement, or ownership of stolen people was prohibited by God and punishable by death. *"Whoever steals a man and sells him, and anyone found in possession of him, shall be put to death."* (Exodus 21:16)^{ESV}. The action of kidnapping to enslave someone, or the benefitting by possession of such a kidnapped and enslaved person was a capital crime. Paul understood and abided by these OT laws. This is why he so directly described slave traders as ungodly, sinful, unholy and irreligious—and therefore unfit for the church.

Encouraging The Discouraged

The church in Paul's day included enslaved and free persons. Paul viewed all people in Christ as equals (brothers in Christ), while acknowledging their social realities—including indentured or chattel slavery. As a marginalized sect in Ancient Rome, the early Christians lacked civil authority and influence, and as such were not politically positioned to challenge the Roman slavery mechanism of that day. The most Paul could do (from an earthly perspective) was to attempt to improve the human rights of those under that institution, and (from the spiritual lens) point them to the freedom they could experience in Christ.

His preaching included radical views that in Christ, the social norms that separated people no longer existed (Galatians 3:28). To Paul, distinctions—such as enslaved or free, rich or poor, male or female—that elevated one group while lowering another should not exist for those truly in Christ. The driving force for Paul's perspective was the imminent return of Christ. Jesus was soon to come and change everything, so whatever status you had or circumstance you were in; you were to be the very best Christian you could be in that setting—whether married or single, enslaved or free, rich or poor (1 Corinthians 7:17-24) — because your temporal earthly condition could not be compared to the eternal change that was soon to come upon Christ's return; *"For I reckon that the sufferings of this present time are not worthy to be compared with the glory which shall be revealed in us"* (Romans 8:18)[KJV]. It was true then and remains true now — our anxieties are too dim to contrast with the brilliance of our future glory with God. But one is left to wonder just how Paul's motivations may have shifted had he known what we now know — that over two thousand years would pass this world before the anticipated return of Christ. And that in the waiting, those slippery slopes of slavery he knew would devolve into such evil forms across the world that he could scarce imagine. But it would be unfair to measure Paul against what he could not know. The pressure test ought to be: given what he knew, how did he respond?

Paul passionately brought the gospel to the Gentiles—a diverse set people viewed by the Jews as social outcasts, spiritually ignorant, unclean, scorned as uncircumcised, underprivileged, racially unworthy, and at times depicted as less than human. Paul became their safe spiritual champion. Paul not only preached equality. He lived it. He openly corrected Peter in front of a collected set of church leaders for racial discrimination — when Peter fellowshipped and ate with Gentiles when alone but later scorned them when other Jews were present. (Galatians 2:11-21). And in the context of the Philemon/Onesimus drama, he boldly hosts, protects, and pleads for Onesimus, a runaway slave.

In our current social context of global human trafficking, normalized sweatshop systems and forced servitude in the Asia Pacific region (the total amount of factory workers in China outnumber the entire population of Texas 217M-30M), and the recent US history of the African Slave Trade followed later by Jim Crow, and pervasive racial injustice toward people groups with a history of enslavement — it is often easy to suggest (from our contextual social lens) that Paul doesn't go far enough on the issue of slavery. In our context that appears to be true. Yet Paul's ministry calling, (much like Christ's) did not include directly addressing all the social ills of their day. Paul focused on converting and maturing Christian believers — despite their social, racial, or religious backgrounds. Paul simply accepted all those who accepted Christ. He filtered all life through the lens of Christ: If you were enslaved, as a Christian you were free in Christ. If you were free, as a Christian you were a slave of Christ (1 Corinthians 7:22).

Slavery to sin

Indentured slavery or voluntary servitude—where individuals could offer themselves as slaves to pay off debts or for other reasons—was such a common practice in Greco-Roman society, that Paul could effortlessly leverage it thematically or metaphorically to underscore spiritual concepts he wanted his audience to understand and relate to easily.

Paul used 'slavery to sin' metaphorically in his letters to the Roman and Galatian churches, and to Titus — so that they could understand the choice of offering themselves up willingly to obey and serve sin or righteousness. Paul's view was that we are by our carnal natures, slaves to sin. *"For at one time we too were foolish, disobedient, misled, and enslaved to all sorts of desires and pleasures—living in malice and envy, being hated and hating one another"* (Titus 3:3)[BSB]. *"Do you not know that when you offer yourselves as obedient slaves, you are slaves to the one you obey, whether you are slaves to sin leading to death, or to obedience leading to righteousness? But thanks be to God that, though you once were slaves to sin, you wholeheartedly obeyed the form of teaching to which you were committed. You have been set free from sin and have become slaves to righteousness"* (Romans 6:16-18)[BSB]. Paul's metaphor not only identifies us as enslaved to sin by our carnal nature, but also quickly illustrates the freedom found in being owned by Jesus Christ.

The Son's Freedom

Paul borrowed this metaphor from Christ. While encouraging Jews who believed in Him, Jesus tells them if they continued in obedience to His word they would be His disciples and experience a truth that would set them free (John 8:31-32). Jesus was as direct as He was clear, yet they could not understand. So, Jesus employed the metaphor of slavery to sin (John 8:33-36)[NIV], which Paul would borrow later in his ministry. *[33]They answered him, "We are Abraham's descendants and have never been slaves of anyone. How can you say that we shall be set free?" [34]Jesus replied, "Very truly I tell you, everyone who sins is a slave to sin. [35]Now a slave has no permanent place in the family, but a son belongs to it forever. [36]So if the Son sets you free, you will be free indeed.* Jesus does not have to use a metaphor to get His salvation point across, but it if it helps us, He will use it. We today, just as those believing Jews are born slaves to sin—addicted to its tendencies; pulled by its gravity, and imprisoned by its darkness—leading to our eternal damnation. Setting us free from this bondage and its resulting death sentence is the foremost desire of the Son of God.

Paul wrote centuries ago to Philemon (a slave owner) about the transformation of Onesimus (a runaway slave) from slave to son. As we read his writing today, it must be with this understanding: Christian believers who accept Jesus Christ as their Savior from sin become His disciples — set free and

METAPHORICALLY, 'DISCIPLES' OF CHRIST ARE 'SLAVES' TO CHRIST — GIVING THEMSELVES OVER WILLINGLY TO OBEY AND WALK IN HIS ORDAINED STEPS.

separated from the bondage of sin. Metaphorically, 'disciples' of Christ are 'slaves' to Christ — giving themselves over willingly to obey and walk in His ordained steps. This 'slavery' metaphor from Christ—which applies to us as well—was later used by both Peter and Paul, and was understood by the recipient of Paul's letter — his friend Philemon.

Chapter 2

THE EMOTIONAL TRIANGLE

The Runaway

Philemon was a wealthy Colossian who owned servants and slaves. Paul visited Colossae and stayed at Philemon's house (teaching for some time).
Philemon was converted along with members of his household, namely his wife and son. While there, Paul and Philemon become close friends. After some time, Paul leaves to continue ministering elsewhere and eventually ends up under house arrest in Rome.

Sometime after Paul's departure, Onesimus, a slave from Philemon's household, robbed Philemon his master and then ran away. Like many such runaway slaves, he had found his way to the sprawling capital city of Rome, hoping to lose himself amid the massive cultural shuffle Rome was in those days. Much like today's large cities (New York, Chicago, or Los Angeles) with their assortment of race, language, and culture; if you wanted to go where you wouldn't stand out, either of those cities would work. For Onesimus, Rome was that place.

So Onesimus has run away. He has escaped his previous servitude. But like all thieves, Onesimus comes to realize he cannot be sustained by what he has stolen. His money runs out. He is destitute for food and shelter. While his successful escape has taken him to a place where no one knows who he is, it is his misfortune that he has also come to a place where he knows no one there either. He is alone. That is, until a name he knows from the past is mentioned. A voice he recalls from his Master's house is heard again — in this faraway city of Rome. Onesimus becomes aware that Paul the Apostle is imprisoned in Rome, and after some time he intentionally seeks him out.

The Safe Preacher

There had to be something special about Paul that caused Onesimus to trust exposing his identity to him. After all, Paul was Philemon's close friend. He was both his brother and confidant. He was Philemon's spiritual leader who converted and baptized him. Their interpersonal, religious, and social connections were well known to Onesimus. Social traditions of punishment along with Onesimus' fugitive status should have convinced him to stay far away from Paul. Connecting with such a close friend of your previous master whom you have wronged, would mean sure judgement and condemnation.

Yet, it appears that Paul's Christlike magnetism impacted Onesimus just as it did Philemon. His kindness toward Philemon was felt by Onesimus as well. Perhaps Paul's attentive ministry engagement with the Gentiles had marked a place in the heart of this Gentile runaway slave. Perhaps Paul's gospel truth that everyone (even Gentiles) can be saved, convinced Onesimus that even he (while wrong and guilty) could be safe with Paul, and perhaps even saved by his gospel. Whatever the reasons were that caused his boldness, Onesimus stepped out in faith and connected with Paul. And this one faith-filled act of seeking and connecting with Paul in Rome would be a life-changing encounter for this lost runaway.

In true Christianity, Paul showed favor to Onesimus and took him under his wing, endeavoring to shed the gospel light unto this lost, wretched fugitive. There was no judgement or condemnation. When a true Christian sees the naked circumstance of a lost sinner, Christ-like compassion overwhelms the heart of that believer. Just as Christ displayed patient compassion toward him on the Damascus road, and took the time to transform his mind, his purpose and his identity (from Saul to Paul); so now we find Paul giving to Onesimus what he had previously received from Christ — impartial, compassionate, and purposeful acceptance.

The Language Of love

The language Paul uses in this letter is intentionally personal. He does not leverage his official title or position to persuade his friend. Rather, he refers to himself as the *"prisoner of Jesus Christ."* (v. 1)^{KJV}. When speaking of others (twelve times) he thoughtfully uses emotional chords such as: brother, dearly beloved, fellowlabourer, partner, brother beloved, and son — to pull on the heart of his dear friend Philemon. For Paul, this was a letter of love. His hope was that Philemon would accept and respond to it as such.

Paul reminds Philemon that in his absence, he still remains on his heart and in his prayers; *"I thank my God, making mention of thee always in my prayers."* (v. 4)^{KJV}. Philemon is loved, valued, and esteemed by Paul. Even in our own Christian circles, not everyone fills our heart with joy. There are some who are more endured than cherished. Yet for Paul, Philemon is a cherished partner. Paul is filled with such gratitude for Philemon's friendship and ministry, that Philemon's name never escapes his daily prayers. This must have simultaneously encouraged and melted the heart of Philemon to know that across such a great distance of space and time — his friend Paul had been lifting his name in prayer to his God.

There is a lesson for us here as well. Our daily prayers must be filled with the names of all those we know. Those close and far must be included. Family, friends, fellow worshippers, loved ones, and even those we find hard to love — for real Christians don't get to choose who they love (a lesson Paul hoped Philemon would soon learn). Lifting the names and needs of others to the Lord in prayer is the epitome of real Christian love. Paul demonstrates this in earnest daily prayer for his friend Philemon. That Christian love, embodied in Paul's daily prayers, would now potentially smooth the way for Philemon to display similar love to Onesimus.

Lovingly, Paul affirms Philemon's Christian values and character. He highlights his reputation of *"love and faith…towards all saints…"* (v. 5)^{KJV}; and how his faithful Christianity in action had positively touched those in his circle of influence; *"…the bowels (hearts) of the saints are refreshed by thee, brother."* (v. 7)^{KJV}. The "saints" mentioned here are 'God's believing people' who have accepted Christ as their Savior. Unbeknownst to Philemon, their estrangement paved the way for Onesimus becoming one of the 'saints' as well. In his opening remarks, Paul is laying it on thick — with purpose. His ingratiating tone is meant to emotionally prepare Philemon for his real request to come.

Philemon had been good to all the saints (in his circle of influence), but Paul now desires Onesimus to be included in that circle as well. The same love, forgiveness, grace and acceptance others experienced with Philemon should now be projected unto Onesimus — the thieving runaway slave.

REAL CHRISTIANS DON'T GET TO CHOOSE WHO THEY LOVE.

The Christian Servant

Paul personally shared the gospel truths one on one with Onesimus — Salvation through faith in Christ; God's benevolent grace; Christ on the cross; Death to sin, and life in Christ; The Holy Spirit's transforming power; The church as a unified body of Christ; and the soon return of the Lord. His time with Paul transformed his identity and purpose. Christ entered and changed his heart. Onesimus listened to the words of life, confessed his sins, and was converted to the faith of Christ.

As a part of his Christ-centered transformation, Onesimus endeared himself to Paul, and cared for the apostle's comfort while he was imprisoned. Onesimus had potential, and Paul saw it. Onesimus would prove to be a useful assistant in Paul's missionary labor, helping to promote the work of the gospel. So much so, that Paul commends and affirms Onesimus in his letter to the Colossians—a group presumed to be familiar with Onesimus' past misdeeds. In Colossians 4:9[KJV], Paul says of Onesimus *"With Onesimus, a faithful and beloved brother, who is one of you. They shall make known unto you all things which are done here."* Here, Paul speaks to the church about the transformation of Onesimus. No longer is he a thief, nor a runaway, nor a slave. Now Christ has transformed him, and he has been conscripted into the missionary work of the Lord. He is described by Paul as faithful, beloved, a brother, a fellow Christian, and one given the task to testify to the church about the gospel events in Rome. What a turn-around!

When Onesimus left Colossae, he carried with him stolen money from his master. Now upon his return, he carries the good news of the ministry in Rome — and He is both the star witness and main evidence of God's transforming power.

Restoration

Where Philemon and Onesimus felt an ever-widening estrangement, Paul (through a spiritual lens) sensed an opportunity for restoration. With his close friend (Philemon) on one hand, and his begotten son (Onesimus) on the other, Paul served as a spiritual bridge between these two Christian believers. Paul was well positioned as a common relational thread between the two men. For in separate times, he had studied with them both, prayed with them both, worshipped with them both, converted and baptized them both. And now as their own life choices and circumstances had set them apart and against each other, Paul desired restoration, reconciliation, and reunion for them both. It was this spirit of restoration that he penned in his accompanying letter to the Colossians (1:20-21)[KJV] *"And, having made peace through the blood of his cross, by him to reconcile all things unto himself; by him, I say, whether they be things in earth, or things in heaven. And you, that were sometime alienated and enemies in your mind by wicked works, yet now hath he reconciled"*; and in the second letter to the Corinthians (5:17-20)[KJV] *"[17]Therefore, if anyone is in Christ, the new creation has come: The old has gone, the new is here!*

¹⁸All this is from God, who reconciled us to himself through Christ and gave us the ministry of reconciliation: ¹⁹that God was reconciling the world to himself in Christ, not counting people's sins against them. And he has committed to us the message of reconciliation. ²⁰We are therefore Christ's ambassadors, as though God were making his appeal through us. We implore you on Christ's behalf: Be reconciled to God"; and to the Galatians (6:1)^KJV *"Brethren, if a man be overtaken in a fault, ye which are spiritual, restore such an one in the spirit of meekness…"* The cost of our sin was paid by the blood of Jesus that we might be reconciled back to God. As recipients of this grace, we (by demonstrating this same grace) must be reconciled one to another. Spiritual reconciliation and spiritual newness are two interwoven halves that make a whole in the Christianity experience. Reconciliation produces spiritual newness, and this newness activates further reconciliation. It is a spiritual impossibility to be reconciled with Christ, but not with others whom He has also reconciled to Himself; *"If a man say, I love God, and hateth his brother, he is a liar: for he that loveth not his brother whom he hath seen, how can he love God whom he hath not seen?"* (1 John 4:20)^KJV. Authentic love for God is inseparable from our love for fellow believers. One cannot truly exist without the other.

When Paul writes of spiritual newness in 2 Corinthians 5:17 (without taking a breath) he connects it immediately with reconciliation (across the next four verses 18-21). These two (reconciliation and newness)

IT IS A SPIRITUAL IMPOSSIBILITY TO BE RECONCILED WITH CHRIST, BUT NOT WITH OTHERS WHOM HE HAS ALSO RECONCILED TO HIMSELF.

were one in Paul's mind. Onesimus was reconciled back to God by his faith in Christ; he was now a new man. For Paul, since spiritual newness had now taken place, human reconciliation was next. Paul would personally put into practice this Spirit led restoration which he had preached to others — seeking to reconcile Onesimus back to Philemon.

In settings of separation, those truly led by the Holy Spirit will always seek restoration. Bringing others back into alignment with God's will and way is the singular agenda for the Spirit led believer. The Spirit leads the believer to close gaps, not widen them. The Spirit leads the believer to heal wounds, not agitate them. Restoration was the anointed ministry mandate for Jesus: *"The Spirit of the Lord is upon me, because he hath anointed me to preach the gospel to the poor; he hath sent me to heal the brokenhearted, to preach deliverance to the captives, and recovering of sight to the blind, to set at liberty them that are bruised."* (Luke 4:18)[KJV]. The Spirit led our Lord to comfort, heal, and deliver the brokenhearted and bruised. Paul followed Jesus his master in doing the same. For believers today, the expectations and the examples are clear. Like Paul and our Lord, we must be spiritual repairers of the breach.

Paul was not only sandwiched between his friendship and love for both these believers, he was also solidly cornered between the expectations of the Roman law and his Christian ethics. Roman law prohibited anyone from helping or employing runaway slaves. But the Mosaic slave fugitive laws allowed Paul the liberty to host and care for Onesimus without the pressure of reporting Onesimus to his master, Philemon. Paul had a real tough decision. Would he obey the Roman law or the spiritual law. His answer (in aiding and comforting Onesimus) was both a lesson and example for Philemon to consider. Paul observed the Old Testament Mosaic law in this matter. "*Thou shalt not deliver unto his master the servant which is escaped from his master unto thee: He shall dwell with thee, even among you, in that place which he shall choose in one of thy gates, where it liketh him best: thou shalt not oppress him.*" (Deuteronomy 23:15-16)^{KJV}.

When Onesimus was spiritually ready, Paul sends him back to his master Philemon. For this was the goal for Paul all along. Though he had grown to love Onesimus and benefited greatly from his fellowship and ministry support, he had always anticipated a time where these two would be reunited. Onesimus could find an elevated acceptance and fellowship with Philemon. Philemon could discover healing when reintroduced to the transformed Onesimus. Once reunited, their potential ministry mutuality could be a tremendous witness for the church in Colossae and beyond.

While Onesimus was spiritually ready to make his return, the question remained: would Philemon be ready for it? Without Paul's intercession, what would be Philemon's reaction to Onesimus? What of the reaction of those in his household? Would Onesimus be met with violence upon his arrival? All these questions (and more) had to move through Paul's mind. So, Paul determined he would not send Onesimus back to feel the heat on his own. He would write a personal letter to Philemon on behalf of his son Onesimus. Having effectively reformed Onesimus' mind, Paul now turns his attention to the aggrieved Philemon, to soften his heart. This captivating book of Philemon is the personal letter of love Paul writes to his friend, advocating the new man Onesimus had become and lovingly pleads for his acceptance back into the master's house, but with a new identity and purpose.

The Christian Dilemma

It is worth noting that the spiritual transformation of Onesimus from runaway slave to Christian servant confronts Philemon with an awkward dilemma. Paul's request would position Christian expectations directly against the social and legal expectations of the that day. Philemon owned Onesimus and could legally put him to death by existing Roman law. Yet, in his converted state, Onesimus was now also owned by Christ — Philemon's master. Would Philemon relinquish (to his master) what was his legal right, and instead demonstrate what was spiritually right? And would he do this willingly? Socially he was right to be grieved, and by the law he could take Onesimus' life. But Philemon's life was not governed by social norms. He was a converted Christian. Having been a willing recipient of God's grace in the past, he would now be expected to be a conduit of that same grace. If he punished or killed Onesimus, what Christian example would he be setting for his fellow believers? He is torn between the flesh and the Spirit. Either he will obey the inclinations of his carnal grief or obey the forgiving nature of the Spirit.

Further, the church which Paul started in Philemon's home has grown, and those believers in the church were acquainted with the theft and loss Philemon had experienced. It is widely believed that Paul's letter to Philemon and the letter to the Colossian church were both authored and delivered in the same timeframe. Thus, Philemon would not only get his personal letter, but he would also hear the reading of the letter to the Colossian church. Both these letters underscored reconciliation and highlighted the transformation of Onesimus as a child of God. The letter to the Colossians would be read aloud in the church, adding pressure to be forgiving. And the personal letter from Paul, his dear friend, would pull on his heart strings. Both letters would work together to strain the grip of Philemon's frustration and soften his heart toward the Christian ethics expected of the church and his fellow believers.

Rollercoaster

This is the love triangle of Paul's letter to Philemon. Everyone involved feels some angst. Everyone involved is loved. Everyone involved is faced with some personal dilemma. Everyone involved is hampered by broken connections. Everyone involved would benefit

HAVING BEEN A WILLING RECIPIENT OF GOD'S GRACE IN THE PAST, HE WOULD NOW BE EXPECTED TO BE A CONDUIT OF THAT SAME GRACE.

from restoration. This precious little letter unveils a wide range of emotions for all involved —the aggrieved Philemon (loved by one, but hurt by another), the guilty Onesimus (transgressor found and then transformed), and the comforter Paul (optimistically pleading for mercy and more).

Beyond Philemon, Onesimus, and Paul, this rollercoaster of emotions is played out in our own spiritual lives as well. Our benevolent God who loves us with an everlasting love (Jeremiah 31:3) is grieved when we turn our backs on Him, and yet He celebrates when we repent and return to Him. Our vacillation between sin and salvation has Him in a spin cycle of emotions. We as sinners are troubled by the distance from God. As the lost sheep in Jesus' parable (Luke 15:4-7), we suffer the guilty agony of being alienated and lost, but without the knowledge of the way home — back to God. Christ experiences the anguish of separation from both sides. He feels God the Father's concerns and is also in tune with our infirmities (Hebrews 4:15). Thankfully, it is His relationship to both sides that makes the difference in this emotional triangle of love.

Summary of The Emotional Triangle

1. Even those who have strayed from God, are still connected to His love triangle.

2. No matter where you have run to, Christ can find, forgive and transform you there.

3. Restoration is God's goal for everyone. As a child of God restoration of others must be your goal as well.

4. As recipients of God's grace in the past, we are now expected to be conduits of that same grace to others.

Reflection Questions

1. How can you be a safe place for the spiritual runaway?

　

2. How can you be a continuous source of grace for others?

　

3. How can Christian love become your default language?

PART TWO
LOVED

Chapter 3

MY SON WHOM I LOVE

Unimagined Love

Paul in the tenth verse pinpoints the object of his letter, His son Onesimus. "*I beseech thee for my son Onesimus, whom I have begotten in my bonds.*"[KJV] The New Living Translation (NLT) expresses it this way: "*I appeal to you to show kindness to my child, Onesimus. I became his father in the faith while here in prison.*"[NLT] Both men knew Onesimus. Both men understood his past. Both men knew that he had been branded a thief and a runaway. Yet Paul is undeniably clear, the object of his letter is not a thief nor a runaway slave. The object is his son, whom he loves — Onesimus.

In part, Paul's letter to Philemon is an introduction to someone Philemon knows of but has never met. It's as though Paul is saying 'Philemon, allow me to introduce to you my son again for the first time'. It's an introduction to a transformed man. A Christian man. A valuable man. A man to be esteemed. An accountable man. An honest man. A trustworthy man. A man in and of God's ministry. Moreover, for Paul, Onesimus was now a man worth loving as a son.

As Paul's close friend, this relational language would have been familiar to Philemon. No doubt he knew of Paul's emotional adoption of other fellow believers as his children. In previous letters, he referenced whole churches—Corinthians and Galatians—as his children, and he as their father; *"My children, for whom I am again in the pains of childbirth until Christ is formed in you,"* (Galatians 4:19)[NIV]; *"...to warn you as my beloved children.... in Christ Jesus I became your father through the gospel"* (1 Corinthians 4:14-15)[BSB]. Paul even took Rufus' mother as his adopted mother in the faith; *"Greet Rufus, chosen in the Lord, and his mother, who has been a mother to me as well"* (Romans 16:13)[BSB]. So perhaps Philemon would not have been surprised at the use of this father/son language, but who Paul referenced with that language of love had to be beyond Philemon's imagination. If the name 'Onesimus' had not been introduced so early in the letter, Philemon may have imagined—in the reading of it—Paul describing some other person. Titus perhaps, whom he calls *"my true child in our common faith"* (Titus 1:4)[BSB]; or Timothy who Paul labels *"my beloved child"* (2 Timothy 1:2)[ESV]; or even Mark who initially for Paul was an acquired taste, but later Paul endearingly describes him as *"my son Mark"* (1 Peter 5:13)[NLT]. Philemon would never have imagined that the person who had wronged him in such a fashion, could now be portrayed by Paul in this way. There was nothing he remembered about Onesimus that gave him the confidence that Paul now had. And yet, as unimaginable as it was, the thief was now trusted. The runaway was now returned. The transgressor had been transformed. The slave was now a son — in the faith. The one easy to hate in the past, now had a character that made him easy to love in the present. Which is why Paul says "*I became his father in the faith while here in prison.*"[NLT]

Paul has managed to form such a relationship with Onesimus that he had grown to love him dearly. He has become his father in the faith. This is the type of relationship we need to form with our Lord and Savior. When we feel far from God, spending time with Jesus is the answer. Through prayer, worship, and study — listening to Him, being taught by Him, and submitting to Him. Only then, when He knows He has our heart, can he turn to His Father and lovingly declare us as His child and appeal for our lives. This saving relationship with Jesus is the only way back to our God. Jesus declares to all runaway sinners, "*I am the way and the truth and the life. No one comes to the Father except through me.*" (John 14:6)[NIV]. We all should desire this type of relationship that enables Jesus to claim us as Paul claimed Onesimus. A relationship with Jesus that empowers Him to reintroduce us to God the Father as: faultless, returned and righteous, good and faithful, honest and valued, submitted and saved — His sons and daughters in whom He is well pleased. Paul does not identify Onesimus as a thieving runaway slave, but as a beloved son. Likewise, Christ looks beyond our past sins and sees us in our righteous future with and through Him.

For Paul the only thing worth contending with—in this letter—was the current Onesimus, not his past; the Godly Onesimus, not his guilt; the transformed Onesimus, not his transgressions. This is a pure reflection of the stance Jesus takes for the runaway sinner. We may be rightly accused by the enemy as sinful and unfaithful and deserving of punishment. But the way Jesus describes us is not based on our past sinful actions. Rather, He describes the believer based on His own past actions — on the cross. His sacrifice changes our identity from sinners to sons and daughters. We are His sons and daughters through His blood. The believer has a belonging connection to Christ by their faith in Him.

Paul's letter to Philemon was delivered personally by Onesimus himself. So, the new Onesimus, standing before Philemon is not only the object of Paul's letter, but is the evidence of his 'spiritual transformation' case — made possible by unimaginable love.

An unimaginable love (Paul to Onesimus) (Jesus to the sinner) has made this transformation possible for the runaway sinner. A love that is larger that sin; imagine that. A love that seeks to redeem; imagine that. A love that forgives; imagine that. A love that frees us from sin; imagine that. Because of this love, we are His children; imagine that. We are objects of His love; imagine that. We are made new by His Spirit; imagine that. Along with Onesimus, we are evidence of God's transforming power; now, just imagine that!

Adoption

The relational terms with which Paul speaks of Onesimus are made possible through 'spiritual adoption'. Paul adopted Onesimus as his son in the faith. While the term adoption is never articulated in the letter, the experience of adoption (personal and spiritual) is woven into the fabric of it — to such an extent that everyone named is described (by Paul) and understood (by the reader) as adopted and related to Paul through the faith. In his salutation, Paul claims Timothy, Philemon, and Apphia (Philemon's wife) as his brothers and sister. In that context, he placed emphasis on Philemon as a 'beloved brother'. Later, Paul stretches further and claims Onesimus, not as a brother, but as his own son whom he loves. He has no claim of family ties with any of these persons except that—in Christ—they are united as brothers and sisters within the household of God. Paul treated everyone as such. If you are a child of God, then you are his brother or sister in Christ. Paul desired Philemon to recognize Onesimus in the same way. A child of God worth loving. A brother to all believers. Adopted into the same Christ-led family into which Philemon had himself been graciously adopted.

Adoption as a spiritual metaphor has four key characteristics worth noting as we consider Paul's adoption of Philemon. First, the desperate need of adoption candidates. Candidates for adoption are orphans, experiencing loss and/or separation. Those available for adoption either no longer have or never had a family to claim them. Spiritual orphans (as we have all been) exist outside of the family circle and beyond the reach of its accompanying benefits (Ephesians 2:12-13). It is this predicament that activates Paul's compassion when he connected with Onesimus in Rome. He viewed Onesimus as Christ views the wandering sinner — lost, downcast, and without hope. *"When he saw the crowds, he felt compassion for them, because they were distressed and dejected, like sheep without a shepherd"* (Matthew 9:36)[CSB]. Jesus was always moved with compassion when faced with the many infirmities of the wayward sinner, and His loving response was always to provide what they were missing or in need of. In Matthew 9:36, it was to be their shepherd, providing protection, guidance, and provision. In Onesimus' orphaned state, (almost as a Christian reflex) Paul provided a place of safety and became a spiritual father.

Second, with adoption, there is no coincidence or happenstance. Adoption is a deliberate choice. No one ever adopts by accident. This is a precious truth for the adopted, for it means they have been chosen. Whatever had been their experience before, they were chosen now. And what an experience for the Christian believer.

IN ONESIMUS' ORPHANED STATE, (ALMOST AS A CHRISTIAN REFLEX) PAUL PROVIDED A PLACE OF SAFETY AND BECAME A SPIRITUAL FATHER.

They have been intentionally chosen and adopted by God through their relationship with Christ "*God decided in advance to adopt us into his own family by bringing us to himself through Jesus Christ. This is what he wanted to do, and it gave him great pleasure*" (Ephesians 1:5)[NLT]. Spiritual adoption speaks to the value God has placed on you. It highlights His love and desire specifically for you, to pick you out of the crowd to be His own child. Those chosen in this way have no need to worry of past rejections. "*When my father and my mother forsake me, then the LORD will take me up.*" (Psalms 27:10)[KJV].

    Third, the adoption experience radically alters our identity. "*Therefore if anyone is in Christ [that is, grafted in, joined to Him by faith in Him as Savior], he is a new creature [reborn and renewed by the Holy Spirit]; the old things [the previous moral and spiritual condition] have passed away. Behold, new things have come [because spiritual awakening brings a new life]*" (2 Corinthians 5:17)[AMP]. When we are adopted by God through Christ, our previous identity is not just gone, it's replaced. Those in Christ have such a new identity; their perspectives, actions, thoughts, words, responses, and desires are unrecognizable to those who had known them before. "*Though your sins are like scarlet, I will make them as white as snow…*"(Isaiah 1:18)[KJV]. Adoption into the family of God is a spiritual makeover. No one will recognize you when Jesus is done cleaning you up and changing your identity. Instead of being identified by our past, we are identified by Jesus' robe of righteousness that covers us

"...he hath clothed me with the garments of salvation, he hath covered me with the robe of righteousness..." (Isaiah 61:10)[KJV]. When we are covered with the robe of Christ's righteousness, God views us as righteous in and through Christ. That becomes our new identity as spiritually adopted children of God.

Fourth, 'spiritual adoption' does not add an old person to the family; it creates a new person within the family. In his letters to the Roman and Galatian churches, Paul leverages the metaphor of 'spiritual adoption' to express that those who are adopted into the family of God experience such a profound social and family status change that they are no longer a slave and have become a son. *"... to redeem them that were under the law, that we might receive the adoption of sons. And because ye are sons, God hath sent forth the Spirit of his Son into your hearts, crying, Abba, Father. Wherefore thou art no more a servant, but a son; and if a son, then an heir of God through Christ."* (Galatians 4:4-7)[KJV]. Spiritual adoption was always the divine plan to re-create mankind back into the image of God. When we are adopted into the household of God, that newness takes place in the mind of Christ, and in the record books of Heaven. Jesus views us as His newly adopted children; transformed from 'slaves of sin' to 'sons and daughters of God' and He introduces us as new and without fault. *"Now unto him that is able to keep you from falling, and to present you faultless before the presence of his glory with exceeding joy"* (Jude 24)[KJV]. And simultaneously the

SPIRITUAL ADOPTION DOES NOT ADD AN OLD PERSON TO THE FAMILY; IT CREATES A NEW PERSON WITHIN THE FAMILY.

records in Heaven also are updated to reflect our new clean slate. *"He canceled the record of the charges against us and took it away by nailing it to the cross"* (Colossians 2:14).

For newly adoptive parents, they may be quite taken with filling all the gaps their adopted child previously had, or they may attempt to protect their new child from past experiences. We find Paul taking on this same mentality with Onesimus. In Paul's attempt to protect Onesimus from the harms that may have been a part of his past slavery experience, and from any future retribution for his past misdeeds, he invites Philemon to view Onesimus in his new identity as Paul's son, thus Philemon's own brother. In Paul's mind, the slavery days of his newly adopted son Onesimus were to be behind him, as his adoption had transitioned him from slave to son. He requests Philemon to hold the same belief and demonstrate that belief through action *"Not now as a servant, but above a servant, a brother beloved…"* (v. 16)^{KJV}. But the mental adjustment needed to be made by Onesimus as well. He would need to see himself as 'son', and place servitude behind him — ridding his mind of the old slavery fears. In Paul's day, those who offered themselves as slaves to repay a debt had little to no social standing and lived under the fear and threats of harsh abuse from their masters. *"So you have not received a spirit that makes you fearful slaves. Instead, you received God's Spirit when he adopted you as his own children. Now we call him, 'Abba, Father'"* (Romans

8:15)^{NLT}. Paul's adoptive love allowed Onesimus to replace 'old slavery fear of harm from an owner' with expectations of protection and provision from a father. Our spiritual adoption provides new identities for both us and God. We become His children, and He becomes our Father.

The Joy of Belonging

Paul requests grace for his new son. He claims Onesimus as his own. But the ownership that Paul declares for Onesimus is ironic. Onesimus had rejected and run away from the experience of being owned by his master Philemon — perhaps any master really. Through deceit and theft, he sought liberty from being owned. And yet, here he was on the verge of his life being spared because someone has now claimed him as his own. And isn't that the way it is with us? Having run away from God, not willing to submit to Him as master of our lives and thus condemned to death for our sins. Yet, in comes Jesus, willing to spare our lives and claim us as His own.

The accompanying angst of Onesimus' past servitude is gone. There isn't a restrictive feeling in this relationship with Paul. He is not constrained. He is free to come and go. Instead, Paul is the one constrained under house arrest. He can go nowhere. Which oddly causes Onesimus to stay — not of bondage as in his previous life. He chooses to stay because he has the liberty to do so. There is something Paul has through endearment with Onesimus, that Philemon never had through force. The ownership Paul flaunts is strangely comforting to Onesimus. No longer someone's slave, but now someone's son. There is a newly acquired light freeness in his steps. He just feels different with Paul, and now he too gladly claims Paul as his father in the faith, just as Paul claims him as his son.

The forced nature of Onesimus' servitude in Philemon's house is of interest — especially since Onesimus now freely serves Paul. Both men have laid claim to Onesimus, yet Paul's claim is more relational than contractual. This created an opposing tension between these two owners that Onesimus can feel. Yet not a harsh pulling tension, but more of an experiential difference he can appreciate. In Philemon's household, Philemon's needs were the center of Onesimus' actions. But in Paul's care, Onesimus' needs were at the center of Paul's actions. Incredibly, even though he was claimed by Paul (as his son in his service), Onesimus had to feel (that with Paul) he was the one being served.

The claim Philemon has as owner of Onesimus is one-sided, evidenced by Onesimus' rejection of his ownership. But the claim being made by Paul is a relational two-way choice with Onesimus. The father claims the son, and the son claims the father. *"And I will be a Father unto you, and ye shall be my sons and daughters, saith the Lord Almighty"* (2 Corinthians 6:18)^{KJV}. There is an appreciable difference between a slave owner touting human tools as property, and a father claiming a son's heart as his own. Onesimus may have been forced into servitude to Philemon—with little or no choice—to pay off a debt or settle some life difficulty. But with Paul it was dissimilar. Onesimus is claimed by Paul, but not because he holds some advantage over him. He claims him as his own son because Onesimus has freely given Paul his heart. And it is this experience of freely giving oneself to Christ that allows Him to claim you before all Heaven and earth as His cherished, forgiven, and saved child. No one can remove God's claim on you as His son or daughter when you have willingly surrendered to Him with your whole heart.

We are not told how long Onesimus stayed with Paul in Rome before returning to Colossae. Nor are we aware of his tenure as a slave in Philemon's house. But while the quantity of time is unknown, the quality of time spent in both places is measurable. Onesimus was a disappointing and thieving runaway in Colossae, but an esteemed and loved son in Rome, and a faithful and beloved brother in his return to Philemon. He was constrained in Colossae, but free in Rome. He was burdened in Colossae, but built up in Rome. He was tasked in Colossae, but taught in Rome. He was punished in Colossae, but protected in Rome. He was fearful in Colossae, but he flourished in Rome. He was a slave in Colossae, but became a son in Rome. He was owned in Colossae, but found real belonging in Rome. Onesimus belonged to Paul as his son in the faith. He owed his safety to Paul. He owed his conversion and ministry future to Paul. Onesimus found the joy of belonging in Rome as Paul's son.

Loving Advocacy

The KJV reads *"I beseech thee for my son Onesimus..."* (V 10). The NIV renders it *"I appeal to you..."* The LSB states *"I plead with you..."* The CEV reads *"I beg you to help..."* Other versions use 'exhort, entreat, or urge. Translations aside, the spirit of the request is vividly clear. Mercy is the request, on behalf of Onesimus. And it is here—with 'on behalf of'—that we find the core character of the letter. Not the goal of the letter mind you, for the character is distinct from Paul's goal of 'forgiveness and acceptance for Onesimus'. Advocacy (on behalf of) is the core character of the letter. Each word chosen. Each phrase constructed. The tender tones used. Everything leveraged here is calculatedly 'on behalf of' Onesimus. He is interceding for his son. Making the case for Onesimus. Advocating for his very heart— his son, whom he loves.

Paul's advocacy precedes the letter itself. His personal conviction of advocacy was a long running prelude to his letter. Long before he penned this to Philemon, Paul was an advocate for slaves (1 Corinthians 7:21); and an advocate for marginalized Gentiles (Galatians 2:11-21); and a Diversity, Equity, and Inclusion (DEI) advocate (Galatians 3:28). By the time we get to the writing of this letter, Paul's personal and active advocacy is nothing new to Onesimus. Mosaic law demanded protection, care, and advocacy for escaped slaves (Deuteronomy 23:15-16). They were not to be returned to their masters. They were to be hosted generously and protected there. This advocacy was what the fugitive slave had with Paul. Paul's acceptance of Onesimus in Rome was an act of advocacy. Hosting and protecting Onesimus was an act of advocacy. Teaching and ultimately converting Onesimus was an act of advocacy. Facilitating ministry opportunities for Onesimus were acts of advocacy. And when it was time for Onesimus to return to face Philemon and potential harm, Paul extends his advocacy in the form of this 'intercessory letter of love' on behalf of his new son Onesimus.

It is entirely possible that for Onesimus, Paul's advocacy was his first experience of true Christian love. While in Philemon's household, Onesimus was treated as property, and perhaps with such harsh severity that it increased his desire for escape. So, it's doubtful that Christian love was something Onesimus associated with his owner Philemon. Conversely, Onesimus experienced Christian love through the care, teaching, trust, and protection which Paul provided in Rome. Paul's Christianity was simple. He lived what God expected. *"The LORD God has told us what is right and what he demands: "See that justice is done, let mercy be your first concern, and humbly obey your God"* (Micah 6:8)[CEV]. The advocacy Paul affords Onesimus is simply Paul living out these expectations as a good Christian. He is

PAUL'S CHRISTIANITY WAS SIMPLE. HE LIVED WHAT GOD EXPECTED.

ensuring "that justice is done," but "mercy" for his son Onesimus was his "first concern." So strong is his defense of Onesimus, that if Paul had been able to travel to Colossae himself, it's very likely that he would be there personally instead of this letter (and what a tragic loss that would be for us readers without this gem of literature).

Beyond the instructions of the law itself. Paul had more personal reasons to provide advocacy for this fugitive slave. He himself understood what it meant to stand against God's will and yet be met with grace. He understood well the plight of making poor decisions for what he justified as righteous reasons. He understood being spiritually wrong while being legally right. He had experienced forgiveness, care, protection and guidance from those he had previously wronged. He understood Onesimus' predicament of living with a dark legal past while facing the horizon of a bright spiritual future. And because he understood all this so well, he could now advocate with love — for the one who he loved.

What similar confidence we as Christian believers have in Christ our advocate! When our records are viewed in Heaven, we have a loving High Priest who advocates for His children by name. As our sins are read, Christ's response is 'they are covered by my sacrificial blood.' His righteousness becomes our own. All those who accept Jesus as their Savior are seen and accepted by God the Father as equally righteous as God the Son. What firm ground the repentant sinner stands on, when in glory Christ argues their case in the Heavenly court!

Onesimus with letter in hand and feet on Colossian soil, stands firmly on the advocacy of the Apostle Paul. What assurance Paul's support must have given Onesimus. The boldness to return to the place of his former shame—wrongly inflicted or personally earned—at the risk of severe punishment or death. In the place where he slinked off in the night, he now returns with confidence in a new day. For the Christian believer, the gospel of Christ gives you something to stand on. A reason to hope and believe in the face of temporal judgement or harm. This is what the Apostle Paul provides for his son whom he loves. And this is what Christ our advocate offers those who He loves: unimaginable love, adoption into the family, a renewed joy of belonging, and loving advocacy.

Summary of My Son Whom I Love

1. God has an unimaginable love for you, which you cannot fully comprehend or articulate.

2. God's divine focus has always been on your eternal future, not your past.

3. Adoption into God's family changes your identity.

4. Even when we stop living up to our names as children of God, Jesus never stops claiming us as His own.

5. All those who accept Jesus as their Savior are seen and accepted by God the Father as equally righteous as God the Son.

Reflection Questions

1. How can you reflect God's unimagined love?

   _____

   _____

   _____

   _____

2. What prevents Jesus' advocacy for you today?

   _____

   _____

   _____

   _____

3. Which past experiences have you've learned from that empower you to advocate for others today?

   _____

   _____

   _____

   _____

Chapter 4

VALUABLE NOW

Profit and Loss

In the eleventh verse Paul employs an interesting play on words that Philemon was sure to catch and find real meaning with. *"Which in time past was to thee unprofitable, but now profitable to thee and to me."*^{KJV} The name Onesimus was a common slave name meaning 'profitable'. Philemon gave Onesimus this name expecting his servitude to be valuable, profitable, reliable and beneficial to him and to the growth of his household. But Philemon would be disappointed. The expected value did not materialize. Onesimus had shown himself unworthy of that name by his deceit in his theft and unreliability in running away. Instead of the expected profit, Philemon was left with a loss.

Beyond the wordplay of his name meaning (profitable) while his actions proved (unprofitable), what the reader and the hearer will also recognize is the audible wordplay. Both words, profitable (eúxrēstos) and unprofitable (áxrēstos) come from the same root word and have a similar pronunciation. With these words, what you read, what you hear, and what you understand is all very much teasingly alike. Through the confluence of these verbal puns, Paul makes his contrasting point to Philemon: Onesimus is valuable now. Previous losses aside. In the present, he is profitable. Quadruply so; for he is now (in his transformed moral state) profitable to you personally; he has been (as my beloved son) profitable to me personally; he has been (through active ministry here, in your stead - mind you) profitable to me in the Lord's work; and he is now (as a proven and faithful ministry co-laborer) profitable to you there in the Colossian ministry. His true value exceeds your previous expectations. God predestined him to be more than a slave. His potential is higher than simply being your servant. His true value to the Lord cannot be calculated by your slavery measurements of efficiency, profit or loss. In reality, you lost something small (and were pained by it), but God has returned something immense (and you are personally and spiritually blessed by it).

This is not the first instance of Paul leveraging the word 'profitable' to define a contrasted view of a person's value over time. In (Acts 15:38) Paul had real issues with Mark (Barnabas' nephew) and refused to include him in ministry because he had deserted Paul and Barnabas mid-stream on a previous missionary trip. He proved to be 'unprofitable' to Paul then, but approximately two years later—in his second letter to

Timothy, Paul made a request for extra ministry help by asking specifically for Mark; "...*Take Mark, and bring him with thee: for he is profitable to me for the ministry*" (2 Timothy 4:11)^{KJV}. Something had taken place, and over this span of time, Mark's profitability rose in the mind of Paul. Mark was even included in the closing acknowledgments in this letter to Philemon. Besides these two examples of personal and spiritual maturity that transitioned both Mark and Onesimus from unprofitable to profitable, there is an additional insight we shouldn't gloss over.

In Mark's story, he's not the only one that has matured. Paul is a pupil of spiritual wisdom here, as well. For Paul had only viewed Mark in one way previously (unprofitable). To such an extent, that it caused division and contention between he and Barnabas (Acts 15:39), causing a split in their ministry relation for some time. But over time he (Paul) matured in a way that allowed him to see that even those who proved unprofitable before can still be valuable in the future when God's Spirit leads them. Paul held optimism that since he gained wisdom from this lesson with Mark, that perhaps Philemon too could learn this lesson with Onesimus.

Rewired

When Onesimus defrauded his master and fled, he fell short of the meaning of his name (profitable). Though, Onesimus himself may argue that he had fallen short of nothing, for that name was not his choice. It was a slavery name forced upon him. Only when Christianity became his personal choice, do we find Onesimus really living the values for the name he bears. When he met Paul, he found a name worth living for — Jesus Christ, who became his Lord and Savior. The name of Jesus written on the heart of Onesimus was no coincidence. God gave Christ a name above all names (Philippians 2:9-11). Jesus then chose Paul to declare His name to the Gentiles (Acts 9:15). Paul then proclaimed "...*everyone who calls on the name of the Lord will be saved*" (Romans 10:13)^{NIV}. Onesimus was taught these gospel truths one-on-one by Paul, and the truth of Christ was branded in his mind, and he gave his heart to the Lord.

Whether with intention or not, Onesimus did not previously live up to his name while in Colossae. He was not a profitable investment for Philemon. His master gave him a name with meaning, but he fell short of it. And so too is it for many of us who claim Christ and His name; claiming Christianity but falling short of the values we espouse and in so doing, proving ourselves unworthy of the name Christian. In his letter to the Romans Paul notes his repeated failures in attempting to live up to the Christian name (Romans 7:14-25). This wasn't a young or inexperienced Paul. This was a seasoned preacher, teacher, and missionary — approximately 17-19 years into his Christian ministry (33-36 AD Damascus Road to 57 AD Letter to the Romans) while in Corinth on his third mission journey. And even with all of his esteemed ministry experience, missionary activity, and Christian knowledge, Paul still had difficulty walking as a Christian should. In bewildered regret he would state: "...*I do not understand my own actions...*" (Romans 7:15)^{ESV}, "*I want to do what is good, but I don't. I don't want to do what is wrong, but I do it anyway.*" (Romans 7:19)^{NLT}, "*So this is the principle I have discovered: When I want to do good, evil is right there with me.*" (Romans 7:21)^{BSB}.

In consideration of this internal Christian struggle, a longtime mentor of mine, Dr. Pete Palmer had this school of thought on Paul's behavioral struggles: What Paul in his frustration could not articulate is that his neural pathways—which dictate his responses and actions— were set and engrained before his Christian conversion. In the past, if anger caused him to yell; the more he repeated yelling in those circumstances, the more engrained that neural pathway was. If in the past, when confronted with embarrassing criticism, he would lie to protect himself; repeating that response set those neural pathways. In his carnal state, when triggered, he would respond based on his engrained neural pathways. Now in his converted state, he had a heart to serve God, but his responses were dictated by his already set neural pathways. What's a Christian to do? Palmer's answer to this Christian behavior dilemma is to allow the Holy Spirit to rewire your mind by setting new neural pathways. When new neural pathways are set by God's Spirit, anger may lead to prayer instead of shouting, and criticism may lead to grace and forgiveness instead of dishonest defense.

Christians today find themselves vacillating between their Christian ethics and carnal desires. Sinful inclinations create and deepen neural pathways that lead to destruction and keep us stuck in unhealthy behaviors and actions. The spirit is willing, but the neural pathways are set. Iniquity is found in our behaviour, because it was engrained in our minds. And this is the challenge today's Christian believer is faced with. However, like Onesimus, you are not too far gone. You can be rewired in your mind. For Onesimus, that included spending time with Paul and allowing the gospel truths to retrain his mind. For us today that means spending time with Jesus and allowing His Spirit to sanctify us. One of the main points of Paul's fruit of the Spirit teaching in Galatians, is that once the Spirit resides in you — He is allowed, enabled, and empowered to rewire your responses to life.

We need to create new neural pathways so that: when we're anxious — we turn to prayer; when we're overwhelmed — we turn to worship; and when we're unsure — we turn to God's scriptures. We need new neural pathways that send us to God for everything! We need to retrain and rewire our thoughts and responses so we can have healthy neural pathways that lead to loving, patient, kind and morally excellent responses.

The willingness of Onesimus to return to Philemon and face triggering circumstances and actions that may have previously resulted in his anger, resentment, or evil

ONCE THE SPIRIT RESIDES IN YOU HE IS ALLOWED, ENABLED, AND EMPOWERED TO REWIRE YOUR RESPONSES TO LIFE.

scheming, seems to serve as sufficient proof—to the reader and hearers in Philemon's house, and for us today—that the Holy Spirit's transforming power had indeed begun rewiring Onesimus' mind with new neural pathways. This allowed him to demonstrate how a real Christian faithfully stands firm in the face of adversity.

Onesimus lived up to his Christian name. It is this worthy name (Christ) which causes believers from every background or life circumstance to stand with their backs straight, and their chins up, and their chests out — filled with a spiritual confidence not native to our sinful world. While Christianity is a daily struggle to live the aspirational ideals of Christ, each Christian believer (including Onesimus) would confess that standing for the name of Christ is the most honorable and internally rewarding experience one can engage in. This Christian walk became Onesimus' daily experience. He was no longer solely identified by (Onesimus) a name given by an owner, now he brandished a new name (Christian) — a descriptor designated to him by his loving Lord.

Both narratives from Paul (that of Onesimus and Paul himself) provide a combined template for today's Christian believer. Though Paul lacked the neuroscience insights to understand just how his own neural pathways were hindering his moral and spiritual progress; he accepted his weaknesses but remained resolute in his mind (Romans 7:25) to strive to live a Christian life that pleased God. Onesimus for his part, allowed the Holy Spirit to rewire his thinking (Romans 12:2), replacing carnal desires with a demonstrated life of Spirit-led Christian values. From these two, we find our own answers for elevated Christian living today.

Choreographed

Onesimus is transformed. Paul is advocating. Philemon is deciding. Yet, amid all of this human effort, what ought not be missed is what God had been doing. Before Onesimus' transformation, God had already decided Onesimus was valuable to Him. It is because God placed such value on Onesimus that Paul (as God's interceding minister) advocates for Onesimus and calls him "profitable." Long before Philemon felt the sting of Onesimus' departure, God had already covered Onesimus with His love and determined to guide him safely to Paul in Rome for ministry preparation. Well before either of these three men met each other, God had already placed His love on them, determined their heavenly value, and ordained their ministry steps in the furtherance of His salvation plan. Though they had not known it beforehand, these three men were saved (in part) to save others — and perhaps each other.

That they individually pushed against God's plan for their own ministry lives (in different ways) didn't matter or alter God's plans in the least. He allowed their free will without adjusting His divine will. Paul persecuted the church, but he was turned around at God's perfect time. Onesimus was a thieving and troubled fugitive, but was transformed and turned around in the place and time of

THOUGH THEY HAD NOT KNOWN IT BEFOREHAND, THESE THREE MEN WERE SAVED (IN PART) TO SAVE OTHERS — AND PERHAPS EACH OTHER.

God's choosing. Philemon, the last of the three sat in the valley of decision as his acceptance of classism, slavery, and human injustice pushed against the grain of the brotherly love and Christian ethics God and the church expected. God's hand was actively moving in their lives — at differing and intersecting times — but toward the same end.

When we elevate this narrative spiritually, we see God's love played out in our own lives. Just as with Paul, Onesimus, and Philemon, God's salvation timing in our lives is simply remarkable. He loved us before we could love Him. *"Even when we were dead in sins"* God *"quickened us together with Christ."* (Ephesians 2:5)^{KJV}. He did not wait for us to be perfect. He loved and saved us before we knew or worshiped Him. While we were lost in our sinful actions, thoughts, and desires; God 'quickened' us — meaning, He brought us back to life spiritually. So, while we are crippled by sin and deserving of eternal death — God provides forgiveness and empowers us to be resurrected back to spiritual life through Jesus Christ. Onesimus experienced this grace just as we do today. Connection with sin results in spiritual death. Connection with Christ results in spiritual life. Onesimus shows us God's transforming grace is available for those who intentionally connect with Christ.

Divine Confidence

The letter is too brief to hold all that Paul feels for and about Onesimus. If Paul were not imprisoned, one can imagine (from this letter) the face-to-face dialogue with Philemon: 'I know he was useless before, but now after some time with me, we've talked at length. He has listened, studied, learned. His mind is new. There is a new spirit within him. He's a new man. The old Onesimus is past — and behold — he is become new. He had run away from servitude — but now he lives to serve God. He is now of great value. To you and to me!'

In quite the same way that Onesimus did not live up to the name given by his master, so too is it for many of us who claim Christ and His name. Claiming Christianity but falling short of the values we espouse and, in so doing, proving ourselves unworthy of the name Christian. How wonderful it would be to know that Jesus has the confidence to vouch for us too in this way? You can almost hear His passionate plea, 'Father, they have spent time with me. We've talked at length and they have listened, studied, and learned. Their minds are new. The Holy Spirit is within them. They die daily to the sins of the world. The old things are passed away – and behold all things are new in their lives. Now they are of great value, to you and to me.'

Profitable is what Onesimus became once the light of the gospel was shed on him. The same is true for you and me. When we come back into a relationship with Christ, dedicating our lives to Him – then we become useful tools for God, valuable enough to be returned to the master's house.

Reappraisal

Both Philemon and Paul had opportunity to invest in Onesimus, yet with opposite results. Onesimus was a disappointment until he gave his heart to Jesus. Paul was now able to vouch for Onesimus because of the difference he saw in him over time. The unprofitable Onesimus was gone. By God's grace Onesimus was a new man who now lived to serve the Lord.

What the Lord and Paul recognized and accepted about Onesimus could now be readily seen by others. His life reflected the character of Christ, and he was also valuable to those around him — especially those in Rome whom he ministered to and with. As a believing Christian Onesimus now aimed to glorify God in all areas of his life, and now everyone who saw or engaged with Onesimus sensed and experienced the brotherly love, kindness, patience, and peace that formed his new life. No doubt Onesimus has learned from Paul the Christian principle he taught the Corinthians "...*whatsoever ye do, do all to the glory of God.*" (1 Corinthians 10:31)[KJV]. Those in Colossae who knew him before have never met this version of Onesimus. His change in temperament, language, and Christian attitude were a welcome surprise.

For the members of Philemon's household and the Colossian church, the reappraisal of Onesimus was a powerful demonstration of God's power to transform lives. The worst his previous reputation was in their minds, the grander the testimony of his change was for God. In Rome he glorified God through active service. But now upon his return, all Onesimus needed to do was show up in his new Christian character and God was glorified and praised as a transformer of men.

Summary of Valuable Now

1. God allows your free will without adjusting His divine will.

2. God has already choreographed a salvation journey for you which takes into account all the detours you will take.

3. The Holy Spirit can help you to create new neural pathways that rewire your mind and your responses.

4. When you give yourself back to Jesus, everyone else will recognize the new person you have become.

5. Your profitability and value to God increases as you spend more intentional time with Jesus.

Reflection Questions

1. Are you living up to your Christian name today?

   _____
   _____
   _____
   _____

2. Have you given Jesus the confidence to vouch for you in the way Paul did for Onesimus?

   _____
   _____
   _____
   _____

3. Can you see where God has created paths for you to return to Him?

   _____
   _____
   _____
   _____

Chapter 5

MY HEART

Poured Out

In this letter his heart is poured out on parchment to his friend Philemon. It could not be more personal. It could not be more tender-hearted. It could not be more meaningful for Paul. Now in receipt of Paul's heart on parchment and in person (through Onesimus), consider the scene Philemon is confronted with. Onesimus' appearance is sudden, surprising, and triggering. He is pleased to hear from Paul, but not so pleased with the choice of messenger. However Philemon initially feels, he cannot show within this circle of Christian witnesses. This is no private occurrence. First, Onesimus is accompanied by Tychicus, a well-respected ministry representative of Paul. Second, Onesimus' presence was sure to draw the attention of the household and even those of the church. Third, Philemon is not the only addressee of the letter. It is addressed to Philemon's wife and son (Apphia and Archippus), and to the church in Philemon's house.

Fourth, silent reading of letters was not the tradition in the ancient world. It would be read aloud in the presence of all including its (previously missing) courier, Onesimus.

Everyone's eyes dart between Onesimus and Philemon — detecting and intuiting any sign of unease. As the proper social greetings are exchanged, an unexpected presence from Onesimus if felt by all. He has not entered this circle as he left it. There is no anxious slavery fright. Instead, a peaceful, mature, and humbly confident Onesimus stands among them as though he belonged. As investigative eyes follow the body language on these two estranged men, the soft breaking of the wax seal is heard with the rustling unfolding of the parchment. Silence is felt as ears yearn, waiting for the reading of this letter.

With tempered enthusiasm and a determined tone of nobility, Philemon's voice breaks the silence. Line by line, his circle of hearers absorbs as Philemon reads aloud Paul's affirming guidance. It is a brief but emotive reading, drawing seemingly choreographed responses as Philemon transitions between the elegantly crafted movements in Paul's threefold message of affirmation, advocacy, and acceptance.

With the first nine verses Paul emphasized his relationship with Philemon. With a confident feel and a pleased look, Philemon intermittently glances around the room while reading the salutations (v 1-9) which names him, his family and his church, and affirmed his Christian character. The tables turned with the second phase of Paul's message (specifically verses 10-14) where he now emphasized his relationship with Onesimus. The very first line of his advocacy, "*I beseech thee for my son Onesimus...*" caused a momentary pause, quizzical looks aimed at Onesimus, a silent swallowing for Philemon, and drew audible surprise from most in the room. Now, Philemon reads even slower and with determined clarity, wanting to ensure he was reading this right. Lastly (with verses 15-21), Paul emphasized a radical reconciliation between these two men. With each phrase and request from Paul, multi-layered questions fill the minds of those present. Son? Paul's heart? Above a servant? Accepted? A brother beloved? Forgiven? An equal partner? Debt free?

While each request is read, the mental wheels of the hearers were turning — 'maybe, yes maybe, I can see how a Christian could do this'. As Paul's descriptive optimism builds, the light of possibility at the end of the tunnel widens and brightens in their minds. This all seemed socially radical, but Christianly right. Everyone is being influenced (in real time) by the two main lessons: Paul's love, and Onesimus' transformation. Gracefully Paul pours out his heart as he affirms, informs, and invites his friend to actions of grace he will want to accept. Paul's heart is poured out, but not in a forceful push, but a smooth and considerate pulling; granting Philemon room to exercise grace toward Onesimus as his own personal choice.

This portrayal of relationship, this heartfelt need to advocate, exquisitely captures the salvific work Christ happily performs for the wayward sinner. His intercession in glory is a pouring out of His own heart for those who have given Him theirs. We can see Christ here saying, because I love him so much, I have given my all for him. This sinner has returned to you at my expense. Therefore, receive him. It's my blood that covers him. Eagerly, He pleads on our behalf, interceding—with similar sentiment as Paul for Onesimus—when our names are brought forth in the Heavenly courts. I plead with you for my child (Romans 8:34) (Hebrews 7:25) whom I have redeemed with my blood (Ephesians 1:7). Through their faith, we are one (Galatians 3:26-28). I delight in this child's value (Matthew 10:31). By my sacrifice and with joy, I present this faultless child to you (Jude 24). Accept again this child as my own heart, clothed in my righteousness (Isaiah 61:10). I never want my redeemed child (Revelation 7:13-17) to leave my presence anymore (John 14:3). As life spilling from the blood of the sacrifice, so we receive life eternal from the poured-out heart of Jesus Christ.

Entwined

Across four verses, beginning with the tenth, Paul reintroduces Onesimus to Philemon, but with intentional chords of emotion that relationally bind Onesimus to himself. From these descriptions which characterize their personal and spiritual connection, Philemon will find zero

PAUL'S HEART IS POURED OUT, BUT NOT IN A FORCEFUL PUSH, BUT A SMOOTH AND CONSIDERATE PULLING; GRANTING PHILEMON ROOM TO EXERCISE GRACE TOWARD ONESIMUS AS HIS OWN PERSONAL CHOICE.

air existing between this father and son. In the 10th verse, "*...my son Onesimus...*" followed by, "*...I became his father in the faith...*" This is who he is to me, and who I am to him. In the 11th verse, "*...now profitable to thee and to me...*" I am a delighted beneficiary of his worth, capability, and value. In the 12th verse, "*Whom I have sent...*" He would not have returned had I not sent him. His travel is tied to my command. "*...receive him, that is, my own heart...*" I am sending him back to you, so please receive him as you would me, because with him comes my heart. In the 13th verse, "*...I wanted to keep him here with me...*" He is gone from me, and it pains me not to have him here. A part of me is taken. Keeping him was my personal preference, and with good reason; "*...he could take your place in helping me...*" I need him in ministry here just as I have needed you.

It's obvious in these four verses that this letter is not only written on behalf of Onesimus. It's written for Paul as well. It is a dual request of grace for this father and son tandem. It's an invitation to accept not only Onesimus (in his new state), but them both in their new faith family unit as well. Paul needs this letter just as Onesimus does. He was glad to write is personally (without a scribe) as mentioned in verse 19 "*I Paul have written it with mine own hand.*"KJV And in his writing, both the transformation of Onesimus and the emotional weight of Paul are used to persuade Philemon. Just as he leverages Onesimus' new Christian character to engender grace from Philemon, he additionally (if not equally) leverages his own personal feelings to soften his friend's heart.

Paul is so very entwined with Onesimus that any outcome—whether positive or negative—is necessarily felt by both he and his son. Should grace abound, then his soul would sing for his beloved son as God sings for the salvation of Jerusalem; *"he will rejoice over thee with joy…he will joy over thee with singing"*(Zephaniah 3:17)[KJV]. Should grace be rejected, his own heart would be pierced as Jeremiah's for Jerusalem at her judgement; *"Oh, my anguish, my anguish! I writhe in pain. Oh, the agony of my heart! My heart pounds within me, I cannot keep silent"* (Jeremiah 4:19). He is so attuned to the heart of Onesimus, that Paul hurts if Onesimus is hurt. And Paul is hoping that similarly Philemon will be sensitive to his (Paul's) own hurt. If this proves true, then Philemon may provide grace based on his connection with Paul — not wishing to personally impact him.

Special To Me

This is about Paul's heart, and how the pulse of it is influenced by a faith-love Paul describes nowhere else in all his writings. Something special has taken place — for this imprisoned childless father and this liberated fatherless son. The brevity of this letter forces a certain truth: Onesimus was different in ways not captured in his letter.

Onesimus' time with Paul was bound within his two-year imprisonment in Rome (Acts 28:30-31). During that time perhaps Paul saw in Onesimus a younger version of himself. Perhaps he was surprisingly inspired by Onesimus' response during their times of study. Perhaps Onesimus' scandalous past reminded him of his own, and perhaps their transformation from wayward to witness felt especially familiar and meaningful to Paul. Or there might be some other context (not mentioned here) for him to be so taken with this newly converted Christian believer.

Paul's imprisonment circumstance provided a unique view of Onesimus' Christian journey. While under house arrest in Rome, Paul had the liberty for others to come and go freely (this is how Onesimus connected with Paul). Imprisonment aside, Paul's abode was a thriving vibrant hub of gospel ministry activity. Beyond Onesimus, other ministry co-laborers (Luke, Timothy, and Tychicus) frequented that rented home, and Paul preached and taught others there. *"And Paul dwelt two whole years in his own hired house, and received all that came in unto him, Preaching the kingdom of God, and teaching those things which concern the Lord Jesus Christ, with all confidence, no man forbidding him."* (Acts 28:30-31)[WBT]. During and after these ministry cross-collaboration visits, Paul could with a keen eye observe how Onesimus absorbed the gospel, engaged with fellow believers, welcomed and greeted them, facilitated for them, and was hospitable to them. Increasingly, Onesimus became Paul's gospel hands and feet (Romans 10:15); and with each visit and interaction, Paul enjoyed a front row seat as he witnessed Onesimus' own ministry taking shape.

The observation beyond the crowds were insightful as well. While others came and left, Onesimus stayed and cared for Paul. Luke and Timothy were stationed elsewhere and could but visit briefly. Onesimus was the real constant in Paul's imprisonment there. When others departed, he remained. Much like the disciples enjoyed lessons of deeper meaning separately after Jesus had spoken to a crowd— now in the absence of visiting groups and ministry leaders — Onesimus gets to ask Paul about what he heard, what they asked, and how those truths applied to his own life and Christian service. Watching spiritual belief and wisdom grow in Onesimus had to create an especially tingly and stirring joy for Paul. Through his love of Christ, his love of others, his humility in learning, his thirst for truth, his ministry passion, and his supportive love for Paul, Onesimus became a specially endeared son to Paul.

Leading in ministry can be lonely and thankless. It can create doubt in your mind as you engage with those you minister to, and those you minister with. Yet, with all the possible insecurities a spiritual leader like Paul faces (with so many against him, doubting him, and misunderstanding him), it seems Paul never had to worry about that with Onesimus. Somewhere within this two-year stint in Rome, Onesimus found an oasis with Paul, and through Onesimus, Paul found his own ministry refreshment — a rich partnership in Christ he never wanted to let go.

The Missing Part

The tables had turned. Onesimus had been missing from Philemon, but upon his return, Onesimus was now missing from Paul. Philemon's 'missing' emotion was anger, but Paul's was an aching angst. *"I am sending him back to you, and with him I am sending my own heart"* (v 12)[KJV]. Paul choses the word "heart" strategically to unify the three phases of his love letter. Philemon's *"kindness has often refreshed the hearts of God's people…"* (v 7), Onesimus is Paul's *"own heart…"* (v 12), and Paul's request of Philemon is: *"refresh my heart in Christ"* (v 20).

Though it was Paul who directed Onesimus to return to Philemon, his departure would prove personally devastating to Paul. In his seasoned age Paul needed the support of others even more. Onesimus' assistance had been a life saver for Paul, and he loved him for it. Onesimus became a ministry extension of Paul beyond the walls of his imprisonment in Rome; possibly scribing, delivering letters, and then bearing messages from area churches back to Paul. Without Onesimus, his time of imprisonment took on a different meaning. As he pens this letter and considers the looming loss of Onesimus, his heart aches. He can't help but describe his own intense feeling; *"…receive him, that is, my own heart…"* (v. 12)[KJV]. My heart is present with you Philemon, but

ONESIMUS FOUND AN OASIS WITH PAUL, AND THROUGH ONESIMUS, PAUL FOUND HIS OWN MINISTRY REFRESHMENT — A RICH PARTNERSHIP IN CHRIST HE NEVER WANTED TO LET GO.

painfully absent from me. Not only has he poured out his heart in the letter, he has sent his heart with the letter. Though the Apostle's death would not be for another four plus years, maybe in this season of his ministry Paul could sense the end approaching. Which would make Onesimus' ministry, presence, support, and sonship even more important to the aging Apostle.

Unquestionably, of more import than any other thing, Paul anticipated Christ returning and accepting Onesimus as His son. Paul cannot help but view Onesimus through this lens of salvation. For Paul, the return of Jesus Christ was imminent. All needed to learn of Him, accept Him, and be covered by Him. While Paul loved and accepted the sinful Onesimus, he looked forward to the glorious day when, having broken the clouds with His personal presence, Christ would lovingly accept Onesimus as His son for an eternity, *"Then we which are alive and remain shall be caught up together with them in the clouds, to meet the Lord in the air: and so shall we ever be with the Lord"* (1 Thessalonians 4:17)^{KJV}. This glorification of Onesimus was always Paul's desire and goal. Paul's entwined faith love of ministry, learning, support, and sonship with Onesimus was a practice run, a kind of road test or living preview of the loving and enduring sonship Onesimus would have in glory with the Lord.

As with Paul, our engagement with the world needs to be a living preview of what it means to be loved, desired, and accepted — even for those who appear unlovable, undesirable, or unacceptable. Much as Paul's experience with Onesimus, it is our (God provided) privilege to represent Christ in this way so that others will know of His love through their experience with us.

A Softened Heart

Philemon's hardened heart was softened by the careful and tender words of Paul. Philemon sensed a peculiar familiarity in Paul's words. He understood—more than those hearing the letter—the connection Onesimus now had with Paul. He recognized—by way of experience—how learning about the gospel of Christ led Onesimus to ministry for Christ. He remembered how spending time with Paul created an unexpected faith-love which buoyed his steps. He understood the personal and spiritual drive Onesimus now felt as he supported Paul's ministry needs. The emotional pride Paul now expressed as he described Onesimus as his "son" and "heart" evoked memories for Philemon of his own time with Paul during their study and worship, culminating with his conversion. Onesimus was walking a road Philemon had previously traveled with Paul. He could understand his Christian journey — and this worked to lower his emotional temperature and thaw the hardness of his own heart.

In the opening of the letter, Paul spoke glowingly of Philemon and his family with love and affirming pride. Philemon found this affirmation acceptable for himself. Now he was confronted with the notion of accepting this

---

PAUL COULD LOVE BOTH HIS FAITH SONS, EVEN AS THEY CONSIDERED EACH OTHER UNLOVABLE.

---

for Onesimus as well. There's a lesson here for the hardened heart. Paul was not confined to Philemon's emotions. While Paul understood why Philemon may be disappointed or angry with Onesimus, he wasn't constrained to feel or respond in the same way. As a type of Christ in this narrative, Paul could love both his faith sons, even as they considered each other unlovable.

Similarly, all those persons with whom we may be disappointed are still able to find acceptance from God. If the salvation of others was dependent on our emotional health, not many (if any at all) would find their way to the kingdom. It is the Christian that reflects the character of Christ, not the other way around. In our seasons of strife, when we see God working in the lives of those who have harmed us, we can be sure God is working in our lives—to soften our hearts in those moments—as well.

These moments of accepting the unacceptable are our opportunities for further spiritual growth which require a softened or changed heart. *"A new heart also will I give you, and a new spirit will I put within you: and I will take away the stony heart out of your flesh, and I will give you an heart of flesh."* (Ezekiel 36:26)[KJV].

Summary of My Heart

1. Christ has already poured out His heart for you.

2. Christ is soon to return. That reality should be your highest priority.

3. When your heart is softened by the Holy Spirit's leading, you will see others as Christ does.

4. Your heart should be so entwined with other believers, that their needs and hurts become yours too.

Reflection Questions

1. Are you able to love others who don't love each other?

   _____
   _____
   _____
   _____

2. How can you serve as a bridge between others who are disconnected?

   _____
   _____
   _____
   _____

3. Have you watched and coached the spiritual growth of someone else? If so, how did that impact your own spiritual walk?

   _____
   _____
   _____
   _____

PART THREE
HOME

Chapter 6
HOME FOREVER

Paul in the fifteenth verse offers a consideration for Philemon. A contrast of time and significance. *"For perhaps he therefore departed for a season, that thou shouldest receive him for ever."*^{KJV} Remarkable. What a tactful and insightfully positive spin on an unfortunate event. The brevity of a passing season equated with the forever nature of eternity. A seasonal loss weighed in the balance with an eternal gain. Yet, even while utilizing these comparisons, what Paul means to emphasize is that—considering the finite loss and the infinite potential—there really is no comparison. The opportunistic benefit of "forever" is tangibly before Philemon. A worthwhile future ready to be grasped and exchanged for the worthless past resentments he gripped for too long. Departure has been replaced with a return, almost as though it was meant to be this way.

Departure

Paul replays the damage but lowers the volume. Not a theft. Not a running away. Not a loss of value or cost. But rather a departure. A wording intentionally temporary in nature, for a departure leaves room for a return. Further, his departure is depicted as a season of predictable transience. A phase one passes through. A dark night of loss unsurprisingly interrupted by the dawn, and with promises of a new day. Paul speaks of the departure as having only a fleeting and/or evaporating significance — justifying Onesimus' past absence as a short (but perhaps necessary) prelude to a brighter and more enduring future.

For those who have spent time with Christ through prayer, study and worship, we can hear Christ interceding for us with the same optimistic tone as Paul pleads for Onesimus: I know you have felt loss. I know that you were wronged. But what that means is that the servants you had then were of no good. But perhaps it was good that they were separated from you for a little while. For in their departure, I have met them. And over time with me they have become the kind of servants who will never leave you again. *"God planned for us to do good things and to live as he has always wanted us to live. This is why he sent Christ to make us what we are."* (Ephesians 2:10)[CEV]. There is nothing like time with Christ so He can change our minds and hearts and remake us into dedicated servants of God — sanctified and prepared for His Holy use.

When viewed in this way, (for the returned) our departure becomes a time of training. A school of hard knocks for sure, yet soothed by the healing grace and companionship of Jesus Christ. Akin to teens who depart home for college and successfully return matured, informed, and prepared for the workforce —so too is the departure of the errant and immature believer who finds Jesus and submits to His salvific truths along their wayward journey. They (like Onesimus) can return transformed, spiritually mature and ready for the Lord's service.

The Silent Exodus

We're not told when he left, only that Onesimus escaped Philemon's household with stolen money. But maybe long before that money went missing, Onesimus already was. Perhaps while in Colossae, Onesimus had already mentally departed — searching for the time and means of escape. If that is remotely true, then we find Philemon's departure woes to be doubled. First, there is a geographic departure of just over 1,300 miles from his household in Colossae to the city of Rome. In this case Philemon would lament a stinging loss of monetary and potential value, for both his money and his slave have departed. Second, is the erosion and departure of relational currency — in the denominational forms of trust, accountability, responsibility, commitment, and dependability. Even if Philemon felt or recognized this emotional departure last, it was surely the first departure to take place. Not surprisingly, an already disgruntled

Onesimus, seeking opportunity for freedom as Paul encouraged (1 Corinthians 7:21) would unshackle himself from any emotional chains that bound him to Philemon, and bolt at the first opportunity.

Our departure from God follows similarly eroded lines as Onesimus from Philemon. Trust in God is eaten away by worldly care and self-indulgence. Commitment wanes as life priorities shift. Dependability becomes one-sided as God may not readily find in us the loyalty He generously demonstrates. This of course (much like with Onesimus) does not mean we have left the house or name of God. We may be viewed under the banner of Christianity, or be present in church, worship, or ministry activity — and still nevertheless have deepening erosion in our dependability, trust of God and loyalty to Him. In effect, our hearts leave before our bodies do.

This type of departure is a slippery mental deceit. This 'missing while present' tempts us with personal dishonesty — accepting our reputation and not our reality (Revelation 3:17). This dangerous reality of 'absent though seemingly active' is alarming to the Lord. Jesus speaks of this dangerous bewilderment in His parable of the coin lost in the house (Luke 15:8) and the prodigal's lost older brother (Luke 15:25-32), both of which are unaware of their true state of lostness and thus are not engaged with making a change for the better. Departing from the Lord in our hearts causes a special troubling anguish for God; *"These people draw near to me with their mouth, and honor me with their lips; but their heart is far from me."* (Matthew 15:8)^KJV. What God desires above all things is our heart. If along the journey of our departure, we invest in time with Jesus and eventually give Him our heart — it will show in our trusting His will, our loyalty to His law, our reflection of His love and grace, and our commitment and dependability in His service.

Divine Choice

The comparison of the temporal (*"For perhaps he therefore departed for a season…"*) vs. the eternal view (*"…that thou shouldest receive him for ever."*) intimates the providence of God in this love triangle. Thus far, Paul had used human emotion, relation, and connection to make his points. But now God's eternal love and divine plans are hinted at. The insertion of divine hands at work in his life would give Philemon emotional pause and spur a different type of reasoning. While Philemon could be justifiably angry with Onesimus' previous actions, or even disappointed with Paul's current request of grace — as a Christian believer it would be hard to be frustrated with God's will. As a believing Christian, Paul expected that Philemon's response to God's hand in his life (during prosperity or pressure) would be to trust the Lord's actions and lean to His guidance. This was the wisdom Solomon invited Philemon and all his readers to accept; *"Trust in the LORD with all thine heart; and lean not unto thine own understanding. In all thy ways acknowledge him, and he shall direct thy paths."* (Proverbs 3:5-6)^KJV. Having been taught by Paul and studied the scriptures for himself, Philemon is spiritually aware that for those who love the Lord, even discomforting and turbulent conditions (such as his current plight) work together for their ultimate good; *"And we know that all things work together for good to them that love God, to them who are the called according to his purpose."* (Romans 8:28)^{KJV}.

God did not architect the harm that occasioned Onesimus' servitude, nor did he construct the harm or loss Philemon experienced upon Onesimus' departure. But God utilized those unfortunate turns to eventually lead both men to a clearer understanding of who He (God) was, and who they were meant to be in and through His Son, Christ. They were not owner or slave, of high social standing or low, first or second class; *"There is neither Jew nor Greek, there is neither bond nor free, there is neither male nor female: for ye are all one in Christ Jesus. And if ye be Christ's, then are ye Abraham's seed, and heirs according to the promise."* (Galatians 3:28-29)^{KJV}. They were one in His planned family. How they met didn't matter. Where He led them did. Brothers and fellow servants in the Lord's work, on a united journey to Heaven. To have Paul tell it, there was no happenstance of Philemon acquiring Onesimus as a slave, nor Onesimus escaping with money, nor returning as a transformed Christian. God is creative enough to use our choices, circumstances, and even departures to bring about His divine will in our lives and align our transformed lives to His eternal plans.

The guiding and protecting hands of God are

intentionally active in our lives just as in the life of Onesimus. While we can in seasons of our lives, describe ourselves as far from God, we can never describe Him in this way. His encouragement to the wayward sinner is: "*I will never leave thee, nor forsake thee.*" (Hebrews 13:5)^{KJV}. Our choices may lead us away from God, but because we are His choice, He stays near while we feel afar. He remains close even as we move away. He is never pleased with our sinful choices, but what Onesimus learned in Rome is that God's response to sin and His response to the sinner are very different in length and action. "*For his anger lasts only a moment, but his favor lasts a lifetime; weeping may stay for the night, but rejoicing comes in the morning.*" (Psalm 30:5)^{NIV}. His patient love in action endures His momentary anger. We are His everlasting choice; therefore, we receive His everlasting love (Jeremiah 31:3). His choices aren't tethered to His emotion. His love for us determines His action. "*If you, God, kept records on wrongdoings, who would stand a chance?...*" But, "*...As it turns out, forgiveness is your habit, and that's why you're worshiped.*" (Psalm 130:3-4)^{MSG}. In God's generosity, grace is applied to the sinner. With His grace, we do not get what we deserve (punishment), but instead, we receive what we could never earn — His divine favor. This is His loving and gracious choice when confronted with our sinful choices.

As starkly divergent as they are, God's choices and our choices inhabit the same space. While we have

---

WITH HIS GRACE, WE DO NOT GET WHAT WE DESERVE (PUNISHMENT), BUT INSTEAD, WE RECEIVE WHAT WE COULD NEVER EARN — HIS DIVINE FAVOR.

---

the liberty to make our own choices, so does God. Just as we can choose to go astray, so too can He choose to guide us to safety. Just as we can choose to follow our carnal natures, so too can God choose to protect us from our desires. Just as we can choose to run away from His presence, so too can He choose to show up where we end up. You can never leave the presence of the God who never leaves you. He is unmovable in our fleeting lives. God does not remain with us because He approves of our sinful choices. He remains with us because (despite our sinful choices) we were His choice before our sin.

King David speaks of this experience with an attending God in our seasons of departure; *"Whither shall I go from thy spirit? or whither shall I flee from thy presence? If I ascend up into heaven, thou art there: if I make my bed in hell, behold, thou art there. If I take the wings of the morning, and dwell in the uttermost parts of the sea; Even there shall thy hand lead me, and thy right hand shall hold me."* (Psalm 139:7-10)^{KJV}. In this Psalm, David celebrates the omnipresence of God. He cannot recall any point in his life where God has not been there. He seems captivated by the thought, and he uses some extreme possibilities to overstate God's presence and guidance in his life.

David uses the polar opposites of Heaven and Hell to answer the questions we may ask in our own quiet time: How far can sin separate me from you Lord? Is there a place where your guiding hand is no longer felt? Can I go too far and lose your loving touch? His poetic answer seems to say: In your life travels, wherever you arrive, God was already there and is still present with you. In the text, David is not asserting that he has the ability to ascend into Heaven. He simply states that if he were to go there, God would be present. The same is true of Hell (the diametric opposite of Heaven). No matter the extremities of his life, whether David is high aloft the mountain of faith, or low in the dark valley of sin; he believes God never leaves him.

The same experience of grace was true for Onesimus and likewise stands true for us today. We are reminded by David that in our seasons of departure we are not so far gone that God can't reach us. It's not so dark that He can't perceive where we are. When you feel lost and far from His side, it is still God's hand that leads you. Not a leading into your sin, but a guiding hand that navigates you to safety, even if that place still seems far from home. Your quiet time with Christ in these places prepares you for the boomerang journey back into God's eternally outstretched arms.

This grace over time was Paul's point for Philemon to consider. *"Perhaps"* Onesimus' departure was an incubation period for his spiritual growth. *"Perhaps"* God allowed his desire for escape and even his action of theft — and worked with the fact that *"he departed for a season…"* so that in the brief incubational vacuum of his Rome experience; God (through Paul) could develop his character, set his mind right with new neural pathways,

JUST AS WE CAN CHOOSE TO RUN AWAY FROM HIS PRESENCE, SO TOO CAN HE CHOOSE TO SHOW UP WHERE WE END UP. YOU CAN NEVER LEAVE THE PRESENCE OF THE GOD WHO NEVER LEAVES YOU.

mature him spiritually, and train him in ministry before returning him to you. "*Perhaps*" God allowed this brief "*season*" of maturation so "*…that thou shouldest receive him for ever.*" "*Perhaps*" his choice to leave was knitted with God's choice for an eternal return.

Seasons

Philemon's time of loss was God's time of gain. Onesimus departed as a slave of Philemon but returned as a transformed servant of the Lord. This transformation would be of great personal benefit to Philemon (should he accept it) but had grander potential for the broader earthly ministry and eternal plans of God.

Philemon had been focused on his loss, his sense of ownership, his reputation, and his prosperity plans — which happened to include Onesimus. But Paul now urged him instead to view Onesimus through the lens of God's ownership and divine plans. God used the timeline of Philemon's brief phase of loss to train, teach, and transform Onesimus into the ministry servant He had pre-ordained him to be.

The length of Onesimus' departure is unknown. We do know Onesimus met Paul in Rome during his house arrest as he awaited to present his case before Caesar (Acts 27:24; 28:19). While we know Paul's house arrest lasted for a whole two years (Acts 28:30-31), we cannot know with any certainty what part of those two years Onesimus stayed with, learned from, and ministered unto Paul. Further, there is no easy way to calculate how long Onesimus was missing before he connected with Paul in Rome. If we made the poor assumption that Onesimus immediately made a beeline for Rome, it would take him by foot and three ships around thirty days to arrive. If miraculously he enjoyed our modern-day transportation, by car and two ferries he would arrive in 32 hours, or in six hours by flight. Of course, the last two options didn't exist for him, and would require him to steal more money than he did. Humor and Geography aside, we simply don't know if Rome was his first and only destination, where else he abode, how long he stayed there, when he arrived in Rome, or how long he stayed in Rome prior to meeting Paul. Maybe he was gone for years or perhaps several months. In either case, Paul calls that length of his departure simply a 'season'.

What was true for Onesimus and Philemon then stands true for us today. If Paul could see the spiritual travels of all the readers of his New Testament writings through the ages; if he were able to understand their waywardness and their life detours; it's more likely than not that he would boil our departure experiences down to mere 'seasons' as well. For Paul, any time away from God is finite compared to eternity with God. Our spiritual departures may seem long to us, but they are but one scene in a long running movie. They are a single staccato beat on a lengthy set of music sheets. They are a blip on the screen of life and cannot be compared to the timeless nature of the life giver. Our seasons of departure from God are just that, seasons. Seasons not only of hardship, but seasons of growth that again enfold our hands in the Lord's.

Fixed

While Paul is viewed here as asking a personal favor of Philemon. We cannot miss the subtle inference that what Paul happily accomplished—with Onesimus during his departure—was also a favor for Philemon. Unstated in the text, yet loudly we hear in his appeal: Philemon, I've fixed it. He wasn't mature enough then, but I've fixed it. He wasn't committed then, but I've fixed it. Whatever the error in his thinking or behavior, during his time away I've fixed it. Even when you had him close, he was far from you, and now in his return home as a transformed man, my friend — I have fixed it for you. You're welcome. Now, do me a favor in return. When he left he was guilty. Fix it for me now, by forgiving him. Previously he felt like an outsider. Fix it for me now, by accepting him as a brother. In the past he was a human tool for your service. Fix that for me now, by accepting him as a partner in the Lord's service. When he was here last, he was viewed as the lowest in our society. Fix it for me now, by accepting and esteeming him just as you would me. His acceptance is a burden on my heart. Until this is resolved for my son who I love, it will be a weight I can hardly bear. So, please my friend, just as I have done for you, fix it for me now.

If we can understand how Paul in this love triangle could ask for this accepting favor from Philemon on behalf of the guilty Onesimus — then we must be able to understand Christ's exclaim in the courts of Heaven (Jude 24) that 'He has fixed it' in our own love triangle with He and God. For those who have given their heart to Jesus Christ, when your name arises in Glory with accusations of sin, He responds 'I have fixed it'. When you bend the knee in earnest faith-filled prayer, begging for forgiveness once again, He joyfully tells all of Glory 'I have fixed it'. When you turn your face to Christ and repent of past life decisions, ambitions, and carnal self-indulgences that distanced you and God, His ecstatic proclamation to God is 'Father I have fixed it' (Matthew 10:32).

When you experience acceptance from God the Father—because Jesus has fixed it—all three corners of your personal love triangle (Jesus, you, and God) become complete. You then become 'one with God and Christ' just as Jesus prayed for "*That they all may be one; as thou, Father, art in me, and I in thee, that they also may be one in us…*" (John 17:20-23)^{KJV}. What Christ fixes, God the Father accepts. "*If the Son therefore shall make you free, ye shall be free indeed.*" (John 8:36). Paul as a type of Christ in this narrative has fixed it, and now it is left with Philemon to accept it.

Eternity

In the fifteenth verse, Paul widens the aperture from earthly to heavenly considerations. He is no longer focused exclusively on this local Colossian incident, or the temporal needs of Philemon. Only if the return of Onesimus is viewed through the lens of eternal salvation could Philemon really appreciate Paul's intent with these words; "...*that thou shouldest receive him for ever.*"

While seasonal departures are human realities, 'forever' is not. Forever and eternity are dimensions which God alone occupies. David confesses this of his God; "*Before the mountains were brought forth, or ever thou hadst formed the earth and the world, even from everlasting to everlasting, thou art God.*" (Psalm 90:2)[KJV]. And Christ self-declares the same to John; "*I am Alpha and Omega, the beginning and the ending, saith the Lord, which is, and which was, and which is to come, the Almighty.*" (Revelation 1:8)[KJV].

So, Paul evokes thoughts of eternity to elevate Philemon's thinking above his earthly realities and toward glory. As a believing and faithful member of the body of Christ (the church), Onesimus was now united with Paul and Philemon in the earthly church but more importantly in their future eternal home in glory. They were bound in their relationship with Christ as co-heirs of God's eternal salvation. "*And since we are his children, we are his heirs. In fact, together with Christ we are heirs of God's glory.*" (Romans 8:17). Through his relationship and faith in Jesus, God had already accepted Onesimus as His child with an eternal future with Him. Now Philemon needed to accept that he had a valuable brother in Christ both in the Colossian church and in their anticipated eternal home.

We would do well to remember Paul's deepest belief was in the soon return of Jesus. Unlike our faith experience with Jesus today, where we exercise a faith based on our Lord whom we have not seen — Paul has both seen and heard the Lord firsthand. First on the road to Damascus, where he experienced His glory and heard His voice (Acts 9:3-6; 22:6-11; 26:12-18); second where he received his gospel directly from Christ (Galatians 1:11-12, 15-16); and third where he saw Christ after His resurrection (1 Corinthians 15:8). That face to face and voice to voice reality—of a living, crucified, and resurrected Christ— is so impactful that Paul expects the return of Christ to be just around the corner. His faith in the return of Christ was based on the evidence that Christ (whom he had seen and heard) had already come the first time. So, Jesus' promise of a return (John 14:1-3) was as real to Paul as His initial arrival (Galatians 4:4-5).

The hope of eternity with Christ was a vivid, living, and breathing reality for Paul. As such, the imminent return of Christ and our eternal future with God became a preaching priority for Paul; *"For our citizenship is in heaven, from where we also wait for a Savior, the Lord Jesus Christ."* (Philippians 3:20); (1 Thessalonians 4:13-5:11); (1 Corinthians 15:51-58); (Romans 13:11-12). It is in this context that Paul chooses the word *"forever"* and he underscores this hope of eternity in his accompanying letter to the Colossians as well; *"…because of the [confident] hope [of experiencing that] which is reserved and waiting for you in heaven. You previously heard of this hope in the message of truth, the gospel [regarding salvation]*." (Colossians 1:5)^AMP. Heaven was as real to Paul as the city of Colossae was to Philemon, and the return of Christ was as real to Paul as the return of Onesimus to Philemon's house. And for Paul, the interval of time between the departure and the eternal return was but a fleeting moment.

Forever Love

While there were emotional bonds between select slaves and owners in those days, that didn't appear to be true for Onesimus. Maybe his time with Philemon was marked with emotional wounds. Perhaps those painful, disturbing and distressing memories pursued him even in his departure, shackling him emotionally though liberated physically. Prior to his season with Paul, Onesimus would never have dreamed that he would 'want' to return to Colossae or the traumatic space of Philemon's house. Yet he has returned to the place of his wounding. And in so doing, displayed a bold contrast for all to examine. For if that place remained the same as he left it, then its threats of abuse and devices of injury remain unchanged. But his presence there was now evidence that Onesimus himself had changed — even if everything around him remained the same. Something had so dramatically changed with Onesimus that Paul was now enabled to shift the focus from the past to the promise of an eternal future. "*For perhaps he therefore departed for a season that thou shouldest receive him for ever.*"

HEAVEN WAS AS REAL TO PAUL AS THE CITY OF COLOSSAE WAS TO PHILEMON, AND THE RETURN OF CHRIST WAS AS REAL TO PAUL AS THE RETURN OF ONESIMUS TO PHILEMON'S HOUSE.

The emotional chord being used by Paul to bind up the previous wounds was love. Through this letter we hear Paul pleading with Philemon to love Onesimus. Yet we don't hear Paul pleading with Onesimus to love Philemon. It stands to reason that that change has already happened for Onesimus. In his season in Rome, Onesimus has learned to love the unlovable. And now if that transformation of love that started in Rome (for Onesimus) is reciprocated in Colossae (by Philemon), then these two brothers of the common faith, would experience Christ's love on earth as a precursor to the eternal love all believers will have in Heaven.

Summary of Home Forever

1. God has given everything He could so that you can have an eternity with Him.

2. Your season away from God cannot be compared to an eternity with Him

3. It is God's divine choice to remain with you even when you depart from Him.

4. God still holds an optimistic view of your future with Him.

5. Jesus can fix it so that all three corners of your personal love triangle (Jesus, you and God) become complete.

Reflection Questions

1. Are you in a departure from God or a return to Him?
   _____
   _____
   _____

2. How can you ensure you are not silently departing from God's will?
   _____
   _____
   _____

3. What has Jesus done in your seasons of departure that pull you back to God?
   _____
   _____
   _____

Chapter 7
IN THE FAMILY NOW

Family Circle

Paul stayed in Philemon's house for some time and had converted Philemon and his wife and son (Apphia and Archippus). The truths of the Christian faith opened up a new world to them. There was a family larger than their own that they could now be a part of — both on earth (with fellow believers) and in glory to come (with angels and the saved). The benefits of acceptance, love, grace, mercy, support, and fellowship found in the Christian family was now theirs to enjoy. What's more, Paul started a literal church in Philemon's house (v. 2), and now other believers would join in fellowship there.

Philemon's family had expanded. And as that fold of Christians grew in his house, Philemon extended to all who joined the same acceptance, love, grace, mercy, support, and fellowship that was unreservedly provided to him when he joined the Christian faith. Seeing this, Paul commended and affirmed Philemon's Christian love in the salutation of this letter: *"Hearing of thy love and faith, which thou hast toward the Lord Jesus, and toward all saints… For we have great joy and consolation in thy love, because the bowels (hearts) of the saints are refreshed by thee, brother."* (vv. 5-7)^{KJV}. All those who believed in Jesus were now his brothers and sisters in Christian faith. Being forgiven and accepted by Christ, they were all in an ever-expanding family together now.

In his previous servitude, Onesimus had become familiar with the household of Philemon. But his time in the house did not afford him a place in the family. He was owned but did not belong; was present but was not included; was required but not desired; and existed but socially did not matter. He was tasked with the family's needs but was positioned on the outskirts of the family benefits. His servitude was his sole connection to them as he looked from the outside in. That was then. But now, presently he had joined the same faith in Christ as they. Now he held the same hope of eternal life with Christ. Now he had been transformed by the same Christ. Now he accepted and depended on the same blood of Christ as his covering from his guilt and sin. Now he lived to serve the same Christ. Now he was a part of the same body of Christ. And as such—in the minds of Christ and Paul—had the same access to the benefits of being within the same faith family.

While Philemon's family expanded, so had God's. With His divine finger He drew a boundary of salvation around Onesimus — including him in the enfolded family

WITH HIS DIVINE FINGER HE DREW A BOUNDARY OF SALVATION AROUND ONESIMUS — INCLUDING HIM IN THE ENFOLDED FAMILY OF THOSE WHO BELIEVED ON HIS SON.

of those who believed on His Son. Onesimus was in the family circle drawn by the hand of God and marked by the blood of Jesus. Once placed there by God Himself, no one could deport Onesimus from those boundaries of faith and hope. Only in his rejection of Christ could Onesimus be removed from his new family circle.

So, Paul's request though polite and gracious, was not really required for Onesimus to have a place in the family of God. In this letter, Paul is not requesting that Onesimus be included in the family circle. Rather, Paul is requesting that since Onesimus was already included (through his faith in Christ), that Philemon now should respond accordingly. And if Philemon really accepted that salvific view, then it would be evidenced by similar actions of acceptance, love, grace, mercy, support, and fellowship toward Onesimus — which Philemon had become known for providing to all those in the family.

From Stranger to Son

Their titles and standing naturally separate (and perhaps even) pit Philemon and Onesimus against each other. Master vs. slave. Owner vs. owned. Free vs. bound. Rich vs. poor. Socially elevated vs socially reduced. And yet, Philemon and Onesimus had more in common when you looked below the surface of their social status. Both Philemon (a Colossian) and Onesimus (nationality unknown) were both Gentiles. As such, they were once considered hopeless strangers as Paul penned in his letter to the Ephesians: "… *ye being in time past Gentiles in the flesh… at that time ye were without Christ, being aliens from the commonwealth of Israel, and strangers from the covenants of promise, having no hope, and without God in the world."* (Ephesians 2:11-12)^{KJV}. In the past both these Gentile men lived without the knowledge and benefit of salvation through Christ. Both had lived lives where their aspirations and pursuits did not include the promises of God. Both wondered aimlessly in the world and were lost spiritually without God. They held (without knowing it) a camaraderie of lostness.

Philemon and Onesimus unknowingly journeyed separate paths that would converge in a common faith in Christ. *"But now in Christ Jesus ye who sometimes were far off are made nigh by the blood of Christ."* (Ephesians 2:13)^{KJV}. Both would meet Paul, be converted by him, and be accepted as a spiritual relative of his. In the one thing that would ultimately matter most to them: (their road to eternal salvation), they had the most in common with each other. Both were transformed from 'stranger' to 'son'. In our own lives, we have taken the same route as Philemon and Onesimus. Past ignorance of and separation from God; lost but found; guilty but befriended by Christ; forgiven and saved by His sacrifice; reunited with God and reintroduced as eternally valuable. We, like them, have been moved from strangers of God's covenant relationship to sons and daughters in the family of God.

PHILEMON AND ONESIMUS UNKNOWINGLY JOURNEYED SEPARATE PATHS THAT WOULD CONVERGE IN A COMMON FAITH IN CHRIST.

As he presses his point of acceptance for Onesimus, Paul does not allow Philemon to escape the truth of his own journey. The narrative of Onesimus' progression from 'stranger' to 'son' should have felt familiar to Philemon. For Paul was the instrument of Philemon's conversion. "...*I should not have to remind you, of course, that you owe your very self to me*" (v. 19). It was Paul who journeyed with Philemon through scripture and led him along righteous paths that moved him from the world's darkness into God's eternal light. Philemon owed his Christianity to Paul. And now, so did Onesimus.

Timing was the only difference between these two conversions. Philemon was converted first. Onesimus was converted several months or years later. This timing difference can skew our perspective of those still travelling. It's needful for the converted Christian to remember the paths they have walked toward salvation, and to be gracious toward those still on their own journey. Humility is required for this kind of grace in the mature Christian. In the spirit of that humility, Paul counted himself as lower than all other saints. "*...I am less than the least of all the Lord's people...*" (Ephesians 3:8)[NIV]. And that humility allowed him to value the spiritual journey and growth of others — including Onesimus.

The unconverted Onesimus from the past that Philemon remembered could not be trusted (for he stole from him), was an unjustified fugitive (as a runaway slave), and had imperfections which proved him unprofitable and unacceptable. Grace was required. But would Philemon muster enough spiritual resolve to look beyond all the wrong he knew (from the past) and apply grace (now in the present)? If Philemon could adopt Paul's modesty, he may be able to view Onesimus with the grace required for the moment.

Considering grace from a divine perspective, the late evangelist E. E. Cleaveland provided this thought: "We are justified before we are qualified. We are accepted before we are acceptable. We are trusted before we are trustworthy. And we are declared perfect while we are being perfected." What a truly exquisite understanding of God's divine perspective. If Philemon embraced this viewpoint, he would recognize Onesimus as justified by the blood of Christ, accepted as righteous through Christ, trusted by Christ, and perfect in Christ — even with his human imperfections. It is through this divine grace that Philemon, Onesimus, and we today are brought from 'strangers' to 'children' of the Living God.

Above a Servant

Of all the parables taught by Jesus, my most cherished is that of the prodigal son in Luke 15:11-32. This unnamed son has much in common with Onesimus the slave. While at home, both felt restrained. Both desired freedom. Both departed. Both were transformed during their departures. Both returned, but as different men than when they left. Both are partially welcomed upon returning: (The father celebrates the prodigal son.

The older brother rejects him. But the father pleads with the older brother — advocating for the returned prodigal) (Paul accepts Onesimus. At best, Philemon is on the fence. Paul pleads with Philemon — advocating for the returned Onesimus). The narrative harmonization between these two salvation stories is incredible — and it may be why I am so drawn to them as my favorite parable and book in the Bible.

Servitude becomes yet another connecting point between these two salvation stories. The prodigal left as a son, but upon his return, he requests to be accepted as a servant. In Luke 15:19 he rehearses his concocted lines — begging his father for a place of servitude in his household. But before the rehearsed words are able to escape his lips (Luke 15:21-22), the father commands that the best robe be put on him (for us and Onesimus, the robe of Jesus' righteousness is the 'best robe'); that shoes be put on his feet (for only family members wore shoes); and that a ring be placed on his finger (signifying his authentic family authority). In this way, everyone would identify and accept him as the father's son. Onesimus left as a servant, but upon his return, Paul requests that he be accepted as his son in the faith. Both of these men returned and were accepted into the family — with the future idea or past reality of servitude being ushered silently behind them.

In the sixteenth verse Paul introduces three characteristics of change that impacts the servitude state of Onesimus: First, no longer a servant. Second, now a brother. Third, a beloved brother. *"Not now as a servant, but above a servant, a brother beloved, specially to me, but how much more unto thee, both in the flesh, and in the Lord?"* (v. 16)^{KJV}. This change of status for Onesimus dictated a change in response by Philemon. By law, Onesimus remains a slave, but Philemon should no longer treat him as such. For Paul is sending him back to where he was, not to who he was. Any other response by Philemon would not reflect the loving response Jesus has toward the repentant sinner. Born and shaped in iniquity, Onesimus was a sinner by nature, but saved by Jesus. In the mind of Christ, he is a sinner but will no longer be treated as one. *"He does not treat us as our sins deserve or repay us according to our iniquities. For as high as the heavens are above the earth, so great is his love for those who fear him; as far as the east is from the west, so far has he removed our transgressions from us."* (Psalms 103:10-12)^{NIV}.

    Much like Philemon, we must change our minds about the people God has changed. When they are forgiven by Him and covered by the robe of Jesus Christ's righteousness, God sees them just as He sees Christ. All their sins are fully covered by Jesus and His righteousness becomes their righteousness. It is in this spiritual context that Paul requests that Onesimus be both seen and accepted above and beyond his previous status or faults.

PAUL IS SENDING HIM BACK TO WHERE HE WAS, NOT TO WHO HE WAS.

Beloved Brother

We can find nowhere else in the New Testament writings—other than this letter of Philemon—where a slave is described as a brother to someone other than another slave. "*...above a servant, a brother beloved, specially to me, but how much more unto thee, both in the flesh, and in the Lord?*" (v. 16). The unique weight of Paul's suggestion is socially immeasurable. Slaves by Roman law were property, not persons. Paul's suggestion travels well beyond the edge of local traditional reasoning. Were he unknown to Philemon, his suggestion would make him appear psychologically compromised. This wasn't a simple concept of upgrading a person from one social status to another. This was suggesting the actual transformation of 'property' into a 'person', and then into a type of person one would desire to hold as dearly as a brother.

Since the nature of Paul's suggestion is so profoundly unique and disruptive to the social order of the day, it could only come from someone who themselves are not governed by those worldly local traditions or thoughts. Only a man of faith could imagine the transformation of an inanimate object into a living and breathing person; or accept the creation of man from dust to living soul; or the miracle of water transformed into wine; or the multiplication of a meager five loaves and two fish lunch into a surplus for thousands; or the miraculous opening of blind eyes, deaf ears, and muted mouths — so that they can see, hear and then glorify the Living God. Only a man who has walked with the miracle maker (Jesus Christ) could so casually make such an improbable suggestion without blinking an eye. And this is what Philemon hears from Paul, the improbable made possible by the power of God.

When we read verse sixteen with our spiritual ears, we can hear and understand Paul's conversational intent: In Onesimus' return Philemon, your ownership has not changed. He is to be yours. But your what? *"Not now as a servant, but above a servant, a brother beloved…"* He is yours, but no longer as (your) servant — for he is now God's servant. So, as you are a child of God, he is now (your) brother — for God has adopted him into the family. There is a spiritual chord that binds Christian believers together as brothers and sisters in the family of faith. Philemon, you now have something new. An addition to the family. He is yours to own as a brother in and through Christ Jesus.

The term chosen by Paul *"beloved"* carries even more weight than *"brother"* and the transforming of simple property into a valuable family member. *"Beloved"* (Agapētós) is a verbal adjective, derived from (Agápē — divine love), and thus is best understood as 'divinely-loved' or 'loved by God'. Those described as *"beloved"* are those who are personally experiencing God's 'Agapē-Love'. *"…I will call them my people, which were not my people; and her beloved, which was not beloved.*" (Romans 9:25)^{KJV}. What Philemon and all readers in his day would hear is Paul suggesting that a slave could be so changed in character, identity and purpose by God, that he could (and should) be accepted as a brother beloved (in the flesh as in the Lord); and that the same God who made that transformation possible in fact held a 'divine love' for him the transformee (your new brother and His new son) even before he was actually transformed (Ephesians 1:3).

Onesimus is "*beloved.*" But by whom? "*Beloved*" by God and certainly "*beloved*" by Christ. Yet Paul adds himself here "*specially to me*" and invites Philemon to join him as well "*but how much more unto thee*". Onesimus is not the only "*beloved*" named by Paul. Philemon and his wife Apphia have also received the same designation; "*…Philemon our dearly beloved… and our beloved Apphia…*" (vv. 1-2)^{KJV}. By adding Onesimus to their divinely loved grouping, Paul has himself defined them (Philemon, Apphia, and Onesimus) as brothers and sister even before the reading of the letter. They are first "*beloved*" by God, then "*beloved*" by Paul, and now each ought to be "*beloved*" by the other.

Partner

In the seventeenth verse, Paul further heightens his request; "*If thou count me therefore a partner, receive him as myself.*" (v. 17)^{KJV}. There are two requests in the letter that begin with the conditional word "*If.*" This is the first. And with it, Paul does not ask a question. He makes a recommendation of action. It's not a question because the topic (their partnership) cannot be questioned. With certainty, Paul was a partner to Philemon, and Philemon to him; "...*unto Philemon our dearly beloved, and fellowlabourer...*" (v. 1)^KJV. Paul started a church in Philemon's own home (v. 2) and left the care of that ministry in Philemon's hands. He prayed constantly for Philemon (v. 4) and kept such tabs on him and his ministry efforts, that Paul was enabled to affirm his efforts of love and faith among the brethren there (v. 5).

Philemon was recognized as a ministry leader in the Colossian area and was known to be connected with Paul (who though not the founder of each church there) was certainly understood and revered as the father of the Colossian ministry. Their partnership was not in question and it was Philemon's honor to be viewed as such by others. So that starting word "*If*" in the minds of Philemon and Paul may as well be "Since" or "Whereas."

Paul seems bolder with each line. Philemon can barely come to grips with one level of request before being met with yet another. First, accept Onesimus as my son. This of course comes as a surprise since Philemon was unaware of Onesimus' whereabouts. Much less that he had been with Paul all the way in Rome. With Paul my friend? In Rome? Why would Paul not send word? How long was he there? But, Paul as friend and partner is my joy, while Onesimus in his theft and desertion is my frustration. How could my problem (Onesimus) be now so connected with my partner (Paul) as to be esteemed as his son? All this and more floods the mind of Philemon as he reads. But then second, accept him as my heart. A piece of Paul is gone because Onesimus is no longer with him? In his previous departure my money went missing, says Philemon. Yet now you want me to care that in his current departure, a part of your heart is missing? How could we have such opposing responses to this divisive fugitive? Then third, accept him as your brother. Wait a minute. That's who he is to you, but why should this now apply to me? A slave as my brother? A thieving slave at that? A fugitive deserving death? Has long confinement in Rome and old age so affected my friend and ministry partner that now Roman law and social decency has escaped his mind? Philemon has to be answering 'no' in his mind while reading each line — until again the request is ratcheted up a fourth time, but now introducing God's feelings toward Onesimus with "*beloved*." Accept him as divinely loved. Here, Paul removes from Philemon any room to maneuver. If God stands with and for Onesimus, then opposing Onesimus would be the same as opposing God Himself. Yet, before Philemon can come to terms with both Paul's and God's endearment toward his thieving fugitive slave, the request is brought to a new level now a fifth time. Now accept him as your partner. What is Paul thinking?! I hardly know what reasons could exist for him to be so loved by Paul and God. But I am very aware of my own lawful and justified rationale for resentment. Thief. Unprofitable. Deceiver. Runaway. Embarrassment. He has cost me time, money and value, and made me a laughingstock to those in my inner circle. And now I must accept him as what? Partner?

As tough as it may have been to digest, Paul says if I am your partner, your associate, your close friend, then accept him as a partner, associate and close friend as well. Paul is of such import to Philemon and the circles of Christianity in that region, that if he were to be released from prison and return there in Colossae to the church he began in Philemon's home, all his needs would be looked after, and the celebration, adoration and welcome he would experience may even border on the near side of pageantry. But at Paul's request, Onesimus, the one-time thieving runaway slave was to be accepted not just as a brother, or beloved, but now as if he were Paul himself.

The Bible says that we are "accepted in the beloved" (Ephesians 1:6)^{KJV} In other words, God the Father accepts us just as He would His own Son Jesus (His Beloved), even though, in ourselves, we are little or no better than a thieving runaway slave. Christ says to God, Father, accept this child as you would me. This is what the sinner receives when they accept Christ as their Savior, High Priest, and Heavenly intercessor. Just as the lost sheep and lost coin were celebrated by all when they were found and returned (Luke 15:6,9), so we are ensured that everyone in Heaven rejoices when a sinner turns his/her life around and accepts salvation through Christ (Luke 15:7). Despite our seasons of doubt, disloyalty to God, rebellious instincts, and repeated waywardness — because of our connection to Christ in this Love Triangle, we are accepted and celebrated (Zephaniah 3:17) as family, an heir, and a true partner!

Summary of In The Family Now

1. You are divinely loved by God.

2. With His divine finger God has drawn a boundary of salvation around you.

3. When you accept Jesus, God accepts you into the family circle marked by the blood of Jesus.

4. As Christians, we all journey separate paths that converge in a common faith. This makes us all brothers and sisters in the family of God.

5. All Christian believers are partners together in the ministry of God.

Reflection Questions

1. Are there some believers you find hard to accept in the family of God?

   _____
   _____
   _____
   _____

2. What can you do better to welcome new believers in the church family?

   _____
   _____
   _____
   _____

3. What are some of your favorite ways of partnering with other believers?

   _____
   _____
   _____
   _____

PART FOUR
RELEASE

Chapter 8

CHARGE THAT TO MY ACCOUNT!

The Transfer

In the eighteenth verse Paul shifts the weight from the shoulders of Onesimus to his own. *"If he hath wronged thee, or oweth thee ought, put that on mine account."*[KJV] The tone set with *"If he hath wronged thee, or oweth thee ought…"*[KJV] appears slightly relaxed on Paul's part. Almost as though he recognizes the concern but is not overly concerned with it himself. While he's not taking it lightly, he's also not intimidated by its weight either. This seems all very manageable in his mind.

The use of the word *"If"* as in the previous verse is conditional but doesn't question the established facts. There is no doubt of Onesimus' guilt of desertion and theft. He is a fugitive. He has broken both the Roman law (in running away as a slave) and the moral law (in his theft of Philemon's money/goods). One could argue this entire letter of advocacy is predicated on his guilt, necessitating Paul's repeated requests for grace, forgiveness, and acceptance. Given any editorial power, Philemon would be quick to exchange *"If"* for "Since I know." So, between them both and for all who will read this account later (including us today), Onesimus' guilt is well established.

Paul was well aware that there was still a debt that Onesimus owed Philemon. There was the matter of the money or goods purloined by Onesimus. But also, the loss of Onesimus for the duration of his absence would not be easily financially calculated by Paul. So, the spirit of his wording appears to be, 'whatever is owed from whatever the wrong — I'll handle it'. Paul taking on this responsibility lightens the burden on Onesimus' mind. For now, in his return, justice demanded that this debt be paid and he has nothing with which to pay. So too it falls to us sinners. No human effort, strength or will is enough to lift the weight required pay the sin debt owed to God. Only in the power of Christ's sacrifice can our shoulders be alleviated of the burden of our debt. Only to His Son will God the Father look and listen for answers when our name and records are voiced in Glory. Only He who has paid the debt can speak with authority of its annulment.

We should be mindful not to miss Paul's careful wording with *"or oweth thee ought…"* Paul is including everything owed. Both in the present and the past. If Onesimus had initially entered into his servitude to pay

---

ONLY HE WHO HAS PAID THE DEBT CAN SPEAK WITH AUTHORITY OF ITS ANNULMENT.

---

off some other debt, his previous debt was unpaid (in his departure) and now the new debt from what he stole plus the cost and loss during his departure would be added.

Paul promises complete payment. And that complete payment frees the debtor. As a Biblical type of Christ, Paul's words and intent fulfills the words of Christ: *"if the Son sets you free, you will be free indeed."* (John 8:36)^{NIV}. If Onesimus was an indentured slave, then payment of the debt in full would set him free. If he was bound by chattel slavery, payment of the debt plus the emotional appeal from Paul could open the door for possible freedom through manumission.

Some believe that Paul's ultimate desire was to have Onesimus returned to him in Rome to continue his ministry for him there. If that belief has merit, then Paul covering Onesimus' debt may very well clear the path for Onesimus to travel freely back to his ministry role in Rome with Paul. Either option points to a literal and/or potential freedom. The same is true for us today. When we turn to Christ our Savior and earnestly ask for forgiveness—by His grace and mercy—our debt is covered, our ledger is cleared, and we are free from the haunts of our past sin and guilt. That's literal, real time, here and now. However, the potential eternal freedom is grander with Christ breaking the clouds to receive those saved for the Kingdom of God.

Note, the debt is not cancelled. It's transferred. *"Put that on mine account"* means a transactional transfer. A transfer of debt. A transfer of responsibility. Moreover, the transfer isn't really a simple one-way movement. The balances from both accounts are transferred. Meaning, what Onesimus owed Philemon is transferred to Paul's ledger, and whatever Philemon owed Paul is transferred to Onesimus' ledger. "*If he hath wronged thee… put that on mine account.*" If his actions have harmed thee, "*put that on mine account.*" Whatever emotional toil has accompanied his error, "*put that on mine account.*" So this is not only regarding the financial debt. This includes the guilt transferred. The harm transferred. The judgement transferred. The punishment transferred. Paul will take it all for his son Onesimus.

With this ledger transfer, we come to understand more clearly the power of Paul's meaning in the 17th and 19th verses; "*If thou count me therefore a partner, receive him as myself.*" (v. 17)^{KJV}. Onesimus now receives what was due to Paul. "*…I should not have to remind you, of course, that you owe your very self to me*" (v. 19)^{KJV}. The honor due Paul; the acceptance due Paul; the fellowship due Paul; the partnership due Paul — it is all transferred to Onesimus. The picture of Jesus in this scene is hard to miss. He gladly transfers our sin to His account. He takes our shame and gives us His glory. He takes our guilt and gives us His righteousness. He takes our judgement and gives us His peace. He takes our punishment and gives us His grace. He takes our death and gives us His eternal life. He takes it all for His children who accept His sacrifice. This transfer changes the equation quite a bit. Philemon has no say in Paul's decision to take on the debt. He has only to accept it. When the debt is transferred to Paul there is no debt left to charge Onesimus with. When our sin is transferred to Christ there is no judgement that can be applied to us. *"There is therefore now no condemnation to them which are in Christ Jesus..."* (Romans 8:1)[KJV].

The Acquittal

Onesimus had wronged Philemon, and justice was required by the law. But Paul is pleading for mercy. When the Bible talks about justice and mixes it with mercy, we get justification — whereby, the sinner is judicially approved to be righteous. When the sinner is justified by faith (Romans 5:1), they are acquitted even while guilty. Acquittal means 'not enough evidence to convict'. Onesimus is guilty. Paul knows that. Philemon knows that. Onesimus knows that. Yet, the justice Onesimus is afforded by Paul is not the type of justice a guilty fugitive usually receives. The transfer of his debt to Paul allows him to walk free, acquitted of all charges. The justice Paul recommends and enables is mixed with mercy. By graciously taking on Onesimus' debt, Paul allows justice and judgement to take place — but without condemning Onesimus.

Justice being mixed with mercy (justification), leading to salvific acquittals of God's people could be physically observed and understood during the Old Testament times through three main symbols of God's salvation plan. First, the practice of animal sacrifice for the forgiveness of sins. Second, the Sanctuary with its Courtyard (where the sacrifices took place); its Holy place (where the priest ministered daily); and its most Holy place (where the High Priest ministered annually). Third, the Ark of the Covenant (a gold-plated wooden chest containing [among other things] the Ten Commandments on engraved tablets). God's Shekinah Glory physically hovered above the closed lid of that Ark — and that lid became known as God's mercy seat. The children of Israel learned about God's salvation through visualization of these three: the sacrifice, the sanctuary, and God's presence above the mercy seat.

The children of Israel knew that a sacrifice of life had to be made for sins to be forgiven, "*...without the shedding of blood there is no forgiveness.*" (Hebrews 9:22)^{BSB}, which they observed and experienced in the Sanctuary Courtyard. They knew that the blood of the sacrifice needed to be presented to God, which happened daily in the Holy place. And they knew that in the Most Holy place, God's presence sat above the enclosed law with intensions of mercy. While their lives were judged by the standards of God's law (the ten commandments), they also received God's mercy as He hovered above the law. Anyone represented by the blood of the sacrifice was acquitted and walked free of sin because the justice they received was mixed with God's mercy.

God's salvation plan experienced by animal

sacrifice in the Old Testament was replaced in the New Testament era by the sacrifice of the paschal lamb, Jesus Christ on the cross. This provided a powerful gospel truth for Paul, which he shared with Onesimus: everyone who accepted and depended on the sacrifice of Jesus Christ received an acquittal because the blood of Jesus represented and covered them. The Christian church understood this. Paul understood this. And Onesimus understood this. But it was now time for Philemon (with the reading of this brief letter) to come to terms with how God's plan of salvation had worked in the life of Onesimus. A divine plan that replaced his conviction with pardon; his indictment with forgiveness; his prosecution with exoneration; his accusation with vindication; and his condemnation with atonement.

Hand-Written

In the Greco-Roman world, a person's debts were recorded in a handwritten note (a Cheirographon) by the person who was owed the debt. These hand-written certificates of debt served as a legal document publicly holding the debtor accountable. The significance of the Cheirographon came in two forms: first, the debt was legally validated because it was personally written by the hand of the person who was owed the debt; second, being publicly available, the debtor's obligations were known by all. When Onesimus ran away with stolen money from Philemon, it's highly probable that a Cheirographon (certificate of debt) was written by Philemon, read aloud, and made available so everyone would know what he did and owed. This became an open threat to Onesimus' newly found freedom.

Much like Onesimus, through our own sinful inclinations and waywardness (Romans 3:23), we have incurred a spiritual debt to God. This "*record of debt*" is our own Cheirographon written by the hand of God, detailing our unpaid obligations. *"Behold, it is written before Me... Your iniquities and the iniquities of your fathers together, Says the Lord... Therefore I will measure their former work into their bosom."* (Isaiah 65:6-7)^{NKJV}. This is a spiritual death warrant against us (Romans 6:23). In our own strength we are unable to satisfy the unpaid spiritual balance, yet there is encouragement. In his letter to the Colossian church (which would be read aloud for Philemon to hear), Paul references the cancellation of our spiritual Cheirographon (certificate of debt), *"...having forgiven us all our trespasses, by canceling the record of debt (Cheirographon) that stood against us with its legal demands. This he set aside, nailing it to the cross."* (Colossians 2:13-15)^{ESV}. The sinner is forgiven. The record is cancelled. The debt is paid. The accusations are forever nailed to the cross. Paul's reminder to the Colossians that their debt had been paid by Jesus, was also a personal inside message to Philemon; that Paul's willingness to transfer Onesimus' debt to himself reflected what Christ had done on the cross for him (Philemon). If transferring Philemon's debt was a good 'Christ' decision — then transferring Onesimus' debt was a good 'Christian' decision as well. Philemon would not be able to unhear such a personal and immediately relevant application as Paul's letter was read in the hearing of the entire church.

Paul handwrites this letter to Philemon. *"I Paul have written it with mine own hand, I will repay it…"* (v. 19)^{KJV}. Some hold the belief that Paul often dictated his letters as others scribed for him. Others believe that Paul handwrote each of his letters. In this letter he makes the point that the writing was not left to the efforts any other. This letter he would write and sign himself. Three times elsewhere Paul speaks to his personal handwriting and signature in his letters: *"See what large letters I use as I write to you with my own hand!"* (Galatians 6:11)^{NIV}. Paul's use of large letters seems (to him) to be a key signature of his epistles. *"I, Paul, write this greeting with my own hand. This is the sign of genuineness in every letter of mine; it is the way I write."* (2 Thessalonians 3:17)^{ESV}. This line suggests that all his letters were written by him — or at the very least 'each greeting or salutation' in his letters were. *"This salutation is from me, Paul, in my own handwriting."* (1 Corinthians 16:21)^{La}. *"I, Paul, write this greeting in my own hand."* (Colossians 4:18)^{NIV}. Whether we subscribe to the idea that Paul handwrites all his letters, or that he personally signs them all; in this case Paul wants Philemon to know he can trust the legitimacy of this letter because he has handwritten it himself. Philemon, you can trust what you have read. My promise is true – I will repay.

Paul's personal handwriting of this letter is critical here. For, if there was a Cheirographon of debt written personally by Philemon, publicly posted, detailing all of Onesimus' wrongs and the debt he owed — then we must view this short handwritten letter from Paul as his own Cheirographon of release (a handwritten certificate of cancelled debt), personally handwritten, publicly read, detailing the transfer of the debt to himself, the payment arrangements, and the cancellation of all obligations for Onesimus. In this view, the letter takes on a wider audience beyond Philemon and his household. It now becomes a public announcement to all who would read or hear it, disarming the accusations against Onesimus, and constraining others to accept Onesimus' debt as both transferred and fully paid.

When debts were fully paid, the Cheirographon was traditionally nailed to a post publicly as visual evidence that the debt had been satisfied. On Calvary, affixed to the cross with His hands and feet pierced by those nails; Christ transferred our sin to Himself, paid our debt in full, set aside the record of our sins, cancelled our death sentence, and permanently nailed the accusations against us to the cross. The cross today is a universal sign of our Savior's sacrifice that allows us to live free and forgiven in His divine grace. Over time when accusations arise against us; when satan (the accuser of the brethren) points to our past deeds; God looks beyond the actions of the repentant sinner and toward the cross, where His crucified Son (along with our sin debt) was nailed to the cross. There in those moments of accusation and judgement, hand-written by the blood of the Lamb is our Cheirographon of release, eternally nailed to His cross as evidence of our salvation.

My Blood

This is the only epistle from the Apostle Paul that does not mention the death of Jesus on the cross, and our salvation through Him. Yet the love triangle played out in this letter is the gospel of salvation made possible by the blood of Jesus. If Jesus on the cross is the signature moment for Christianity, then the blood of Jesus is the ink used in the writing of it. In the nineteenth verse Paul pens: "*I Paul have written it with mine own hand, I will repay it...*"[KJV] Spiritually, this line is of great significance. Paul here is a biblical type of Christ. We can hear the voice of Christ exclaiming through this story: 'I have written this with my own blood. I have paid the cost. This letter of love is written in my blood. No one else can do this for them. I claim this child with my blood!'

The powerful blood of Jesus does two things: first, it covers; "*for this is My blood of the [new and better] covenant, which [ratifies the agreement and] is being poured out for many [as a substitutionary atonement] for the forgiveness of sins.*" (Matthew 26:28) [AMP]; and second, it cleans "*...the blood of Jesus Christ cleanses us from every sin.*" (1 John 1:7)[SLT]. Both these actions remove from sight any wrong that has been done. The blood of Jesus covers the sinner's faults and cleanses

IF JESUS ON THE CROSS IS THE SIGNATURE MOMENT FOR CHRISTIANITY, THEN THE BLOOD OF JESUS IS THE INK USED IN THE WRITING OF IT.

their heart; *"Create in me a clean heart, O God; and renew a right spirit within me."*^KJV (Psalm 51:10).

Onesimus travelled back to Colossae covered by the socially recognized legality of Paul's Cheirographon of release. But more importantly, he had also returned spiritually covered by the sacrificed blood of his Savior, Jesus Christ. Like Onesimus, our records of sins are covered by the blood of Christ and by it the argument between our salvation and our condemnation is quieted. *"There is therefore now no condemnation to them which are in Christ Jesus…"* (Romans 8:1)^KJV

One can imagine Onesimus' slow and silent steps from Rome back to Philemon's house in Colossae. Each stride brings Onesimus closer to the place of his previous brokenness. Long before his actual arrival, those dark dormant memories resurface like submerged emotional plaque, built up and hardened in his mind as ill-formed calcified trauma. He wrestled with those memories for they were real; but he was governed by his recent conversion — which was just as real and even more powerful. His silent walk with weakened knees became strides of strength and determination, empowered by God's purpose and desire for him — unrivaled peace with God and men.

Whatever fears lingered (as they often will during our spiritual journey), upon his arrival to his previous abode in Colossae and with letter in hand, Onesimus was comforted and reassured by experiencing a spiritual truth he had only heard read from the Psalms; "*Thou preparest a table before me in the presence of mine enemies: thou anointest my head with oil; my cup runneth over.*" (Psalm 23:5)^KJV. The price of his spiritual debt was paid through the blood of Jesus; and God chose to put Onesimus back together right in front of the people and in the place that broke him. God exalted him in the place of his error.

As with Joseph, Onesimus' enslavement gave rise to his ascent; as he returns now beloved by God, above a servant, a brother and partner to be celebrated, and a minister of faith that will share God's ministry news from Rome to those in the Colossian church. Because a transfer was made; because his debt was cancelled; because someone paid the cost; this burdensome and traumatic place now became his breakthrough turning point.

Onesimus entered the city as one triumphant over the past and covered by a peace they detected but could not make sense of. "*Therefore, since we have been justified [that is, acquitted of sin, declared blameless before God] by faith, [let us grasp the fact that] we have peace with God [and the joy of reconciliation with Him] through our Lord Jesus Christ (the Messiah, the Anointed).*"^AMP (Romans 5:1). Accusations and claims of condemnation were ready to greet him in Colossae, yet what Onesimus knew (and we must hold dear) is that the blood of Jesus will always dispute and dissolve the enemy's accusations and claims.

GOD CHOSE TO PUT ONESIMUS BACK TOGETHER RIGHT IN FRONT OF THE PEOPLE AND IN THE PLACE THAT BROKE HIM.

Living Peace

There was something new about Onesimus. Philemon and his household could sense it from afar and vividly describe it up close. He was pleasing, likeable and disarming. His personal engagement with them felt different, but they too were also different after engaging with him. There was something that not only neutralized their prejudiced angst, but also strangely warmed their hearts. What was this that they were feeling and experiencing with this new Christian convert Onesimus?

Those who interacted with Onesimus could tell there was something different, but they couldn't trace the source of that difference. In his wisdom, Solomon sheds some light on Onesimus' case for us. *"When a man's ways please the LORD, he maketh even his enemies to be at peace with him."* (Proverbs 16:7)^{KJV}. With certainty, Onesimus had been transformed. His repentance, his conversion, and his obedience to the truth and cause of Christ were clear. The transforming power of the Holy Spirit replaced his past emotions of resentment, inclinations to deception, and actions of theft and malice: and instead filled his heart and mind with love, joy, and peace. His ways were now governed by God's Spirit and will.

Onesimus was a new person, and one can only expect that his new thoughts, words, actions and responses now pleased the Lord. The indwelling Spirit of God had been allowed by Onesimus to effect enough change inside, that others could detect and experience that transformation on the outside. His responses were Spirit led and as others interacted with him, they were indirectly connecting with God through Onesimus. Onesimus was at peace with his God because his ways pleased the Lord. In return, God extended that peace to others who were previously not in harmony with Onesimus.

On the surface, much of Paul's advocacy in this letter leans on the relationship Onesimus had with Paul. But below the surface, beyond the purview of most, Paul had identified the perfect reason to advocate for Onesimus — the peace Onesimus now had with God.

Onesimus' faithful dependence on Christ while in Rome, resulted in a divinely infused peacefulness he seemed to carry with him. *"Thou wilt keep him in perfect peace, whose mind is stayed on thee: because he trusteth in thee."* (Isaiah 26:3)^{KJV}. We leave the writing of this letter not with thoughts of his past servitude, nor his thievery, nor his escape, nor his profitability or value; not even of Paul's love for him. The most enduring lesson and thought must be that; spending time with Christ allowed Onesimus to be fully at peace—with God and himself.

Summary of Charge That To My Account

1. Our transfer with Christ means He receives our debt and death while we receive His righteousness and life.

2. When God mixes justice with mercy we get 'justification'. Those 'justified' by faith' are acquitted of all sin.

3. Christ not only transfers your debt to Himself; He pays the debt in full.

4. Christ nailed on the cross is our Cheirographon of release of all sin debt.

5. The blood of Jesus covers our sins and cleans our hearts of impure inclinations.

Reflection Questions

1. Have you fully accepted the transfer, cancellation, and payment of your sins by Christ?

   _____
   _____
   _____
   _____

2. Do you fully accept the blood of Jesus as your covering from sin?

   _____
   _____
   _____
   _____

3. What areas of your life do you still need His peace?

   _____
   _____
   _____
   _____

Chapter 9
MY OWN LETTER OF LOVE

This book of Philemon; this personal letter of love; this salvific handwritten Cheirographon of release — vindicates Onesimus; highlighting the goodness of his life while cancelling the dark debt of his past. What a vibrant illustration of transformation. No longer a slave to sin or Philemon. Beyond a mere faith son of an aged apostle. He is revealed as God had always intended him to be: His beloved and accepted child.

Onesimus left Colossae as a useless thieving runaway slave, but because of this triangle of love, he returned as a faithful and beloved brother, who had been of great service and now could find acceptance in the master's eye. This experience of acceptance is not left only to Onesimus. You too can return home! No longer as slaves to sin, but as beloved and accepted members of the family, forever embraced in this triangle of love with

God your Father and Jesus Christ your Savior.

Philemon's letter is saturated in a deep love for Onesimus and penned to unite the three corners of the love triangle between Philemon, Onesimus and Paul. Today, we are all, in one way or another, wrapped up in the drama of this little letter. Some may be like Onesimus, perhaps still running, still hiding, feeling guilty, longing to repent and to be reconciled with God. Others may have already connected with and been transformed by Christ and are on their slow trek back to a God they have robbed of so much and left for so long a time. But whether in our resistance or distance, there is hope for the wayward sinner. Jesus your advocate is willing and able to reconcile you back to your God.

You can have your own personal letter of love handwritten by Jesus Christ with His own blood; sealed with His sacrifice and permeated with His divine restoration power. Yes, in this triangle of love between you, Christ and God; you matter enough to have your own letter of love. A handwritten Cheirographon of release from all your sins, and a divine record of your exoneration eternally nailed to the cross of Christ—your loving Savior.

**YOU CAN HAVE
YOUR OWN
PERSONAL
LETTER OF LOVE
HANDWRITTEN
BY JESUS CHRIST
WITH HIS
OWN BLOOD.**

ABOUT THE AUTHOR

Lance Moncrieffe is a seasoned speaker, leadership coach and pastor. He has led diverse church congregations for over 17 years, and his leadership focuses on Biblical storytelling, personal Bible study, discipleship growth, and digital ministry outreach.

His favorite Bible story (which tells his life story) is 'the prodigal son'. His favorite Bible book (which tells his salvation journey) is Philemon. His favorite Bible verse (which governs his life today) is Galatians 2:20.

He has combined his 30+ years of consulting experience with his ministry leadership to produce workshops on 'Digital Experiences in Ministry' and 'Digital Transformation for Churches' to churches, conferences, camp meetings and ministry groups.

He provides Ministry Training, Seminars, and Workshops for ministry leaders on the following topics: Leadership Methods of Christ, Spiritual Vitality, Sermon Preparation, Preaching Delivery, and Pastoral Leadership in a Digital Age.

KEYNOTES.
COACHING.
WORKSHOPS.

Lance offers dynamic coaching for executives and organizations, empowering growth and excellence.

He focuses on empowering leaders through executive coaching and impactful speaking engagements. With over 35 years of executive leadership and a commitment to servant leadership, Lance combines depth of experience and a passion for development, guiding individuals and organizations to extraordinary success.

LanceMoncrieffe.com

CHAPTER ONE NOTES

CHAPTER TWO NOTES

CHAPTER THREE NOTES

CHAPTER FOUR NOTES

CHAPTER FIVE NOTES

CHAPTER SIX NOTES

CHAPTER SEVEN NOTES

CHAPTER EIGHT NOTES

CHAPTER NINE NOTES

www.ingramcontent.com/pod-product-compliance
Lightning Source LLC
Chambersburg PA
CBHW070951180426
43194CB00042B/2269